THE GREAT

By Tony McNamara

CURRENCY PRESS
The performing arts publisher

CURRENCY PLAYS

First published in 2008
by Currency Press Pty Ltd,
Gadigal Land, Suite 310, 46-56 Kippax Street, Surry Hills NSW, Australia
enquiries@currency.com.au; www.currency.com.au
in association with
Sydney Theatre Company

Typeset by Dean Nottle for Currency Press.
Front cover shows Robin McLeavy. Cover image by Grant Sparkes-Carroll. Photo
by Jason Capobianco
Currency Press acknowledges the Traditional Owners of the Country on which we
live and work. We pay our respects to all Aboriginal and Torres Strait Islander Elders,
past and present.

A catalogue record for this
book is available from the
NATIONAL
LIBRARY
OF AUSTRALIA
National Library of Australia

Contents

The Great was first produced by Sydney Theatre Company at the Wharf 1 Theatre on 31 May 2008, with the following cast:

YOUNG CATHERINE/NATALIE	Robin McLeavy
OLDER CATHERINE	Elizabeth Alexander
PETER/DIDI	Toby Schmitz
YOUNG ORLO/PLIMPTOV	Matthew Moore
ARCHBISHOP/OLDER ORLO	Nicholas Bell
HERMES/VAL	Ben Geurens
MARIAL/ANGELINE	Mandy McElhinney
VELEMENTOV/A GENERAL	Alan Dukes

Director, Peter Evans
Set Designer, Fiona Crombie
Costume Designer, Tess Schofield
Lighting Designer, Damien Cooper
Composer, Alan John
Sound Designer, Steve Francis

CHARACTERS

CATHERINE
PETER
DIDI
NATALIE
ANGELINE
ARCHBISHOP SAMSA (ARCHIE)
GENERAL VELOMONTOV
MARIAL
ORLO
HERMES
PLIMPTOV
VAL
A PAGE
A GENERAL
A COUNT

ACT ONE

SCENE ONE

France. 1700s.

The young CATHERINE THE GREAT. *A lovely park setting. She sits with her friend* ANGELINE.

ANGELINE: I overheard my father talking last night, he said your father is a fool, that you have practically no money, that you will soon lose everything.

CATHERINE: I don't think that's true. We had strawberries last night.

ANGELINE: So?

CATHERINE: They're an expensive fruit, and I always equate them with optimism and happiness.

ANGELINE: You are a very naive girl. It is embarrassing to me.

CATHERINE: I just see the good in things. You should try it. There is so much good, Angeline. This morning I found a bird in my pocket. A little chirping wren, I hadn't even noticed it climb in there, just heard it chirping happily.

ANGELINE: Oh, my God. You are a child.

CATHERINE: Also not true. I am to be married.

ANGELINE: No!

CATHERINE: Yes!

ANGELINE: No!

CATHERINE: Yes!

ANGELINE: No!

CATHERINE: Oh, I love this! Yes!

ANGELINE: No!

CATHERINE: Yes!

ANGELINE: No!

CATHERINE: Okay, I'm done, accept it so we can move on.

ANGELINE: Who? Does this crazy man know your family's situation?

CATHERINE: That we have strawberries most nights? I shall be sure to tell him. I trust he will share my love of this optimistic fruit.

ANGELINE: I mean that you have nothing.

CATHERINE: He cares not for such things. Emperor Peter and I are about finer things.

ANGELINE: Emperor Peter of Russia?!

CATHERINE: Yip.

ANGELINE: The whole of Russia!

CATHERINE: It is a big place. We have a map, we gathered round it while we ate strawberries. There was also cream, yellow and thick. I'm to be an Empress, isn't that so... completely right.

ANGELINE: No!

CATHERINE: Yes!

ANGELINE: No!

CATHERINE: Angeline, I cannot do this again, it is too tiring, and I have a long trip ahead of me, to Russia. Where I am to be Empress.

ANGELINE: How did this happen?

CATHERINE: He was sent my portrait and chose me. Apparently he was struck dumb with love.

ANGELINE: That's clear. Your portrait. Who painted it, Michelangelo?! He will be disappointed when you arrive.

CATHERINE: He will love me and I him. He has sent me a beautiful letter. Why must you be cruel, Angeline? You are a plain girl and it would suit you better to have a sunny disposition.

ANGELINE: You, Empress of Russia. I feel faint.

CATHERINE: They have bears. I may get one. They look cute.

ANGELINE: Cute... You cannot, you are too naive for this. Remember the first time your blood came through?

CATHERINE: I...

ANGELINE: 'Help, someone! I think I've been shot!'

CATHERINE: I was bleeding quite inexplicably, it seemed a logical explanation.

ANGELINE: How did he even know you existed?

CATHERINE: He is my mother's second cousin.

ANGELINE: You are practically brother and sister. Your children will look like hamsters!

CATHERINE: Then they will remind me of you and I shall look fondly upon them. We will not meet again, dear Angeline. But I shall carry the look on your face with me always. You have been often cruel to me but I have felt your unhappiness and so, I forgive you.

ANGELINE: I don't want you to—

CATHERINE: Too late. I already did it. I greet the world with love and it greets me the same, you spit in its eye and wonder why you're face is wet. Peter the Great, I guess that will make me Catherine the Great.

SCENE TWO

Russia. The court of Emperor Peter. An austere dark room.

CATHERINE *stands.* PETER *is flanked by* ARCHBISHOP SAMSA (ARCHIE) *and* GENERAL VELOMONTOV. *He runs an eye over her.*

PETER: You looked taller in your portrait.

CATHERINE: Oh... um... I...

PETER: [*to the others*] Send her back. Get me a tall one. [*He turns to go. He starts giggling, crazily.*] See what I did then? I'm kidding, kidding...

CATHERINE: Oh, I see... yes... [*Laughing*] How amusing. I got this branch of spruce. It is an evergreen and I hoped it would be a symbol of our feelings for each other. That we would be constant and caring for all our lives.

He takes the branch, bemused.

PETER: [*to* ARCHIE] She gave me a twig? She's not a retard, is she?

ARCHIE: It wasn't mentioned.

CATHERINE: I assure you I am of sound mind, sir.

PETER: Of course you are. Besides, not your mind I'm interested in, more your ovaries and that pink wet thing.

CATHERINE: My tongue?

PETER: No your... oh, you're kidding.

CATHERINE: No.

PETER: No? Whew, you're a little tricky.

CATHERINE: I aim to be nothing but transparent to you, I wish you to see into my heart and I yours. I wanted to thank you for the letter you wrote me. It warmed my heart, noble poetic sentiments. I felt the same as you, that our love will grow from that small ember to a blaze that will warm our whole kingdom.

PETER: I wrote a letter?

ARCHIE: We threw together a little something. Dostovey did it.

PETER: The long-haired guy who smells like cheese?

ARCHIE: Yes.

PETER: How 'bout that. Well, you liked it, so that's grand. Did you have a good trip?

CATHERINE: I saw men coming back on the road, soldiers.

PETER: Oh, did they look happy?

CATHERINE: No, there were many terrible wounds, a sense of despair that seemed to permeate the air like the flies that followed them in swarms.

PETER: Shit, maybe we lost. Velomontov, you horse's bitch!

VELOMONTOV: Sir, I have had no reports.

> PETER *kicks him.*

PETER: Get to the map room, fat boy. [*To* CATHERINE] Anyway, great that you're here.

CATHERINE: I hope I make you happy.

PETER: You're perfect.

CATHERINE: Thank you.

PETER: I need a queen who's from aristocracy but not a family that is any way powerful or a player, your family apparently are fucked. I wish Mother was here. I miss her.

CATHERINE: That's sweet.

PETER: You smell funny, is that usual?

CATHERINE: I... have been travelling.

PETER: Let's hope that's it. Wedding's at seven. Man, you're cute. The Archbishop will now give you some instructions on the day's events. I have to go back to my whores... horses. Horses. Going riding.

He starts laughing hysterically. He exits, leaving her with ARCHIE, MARIAL *and a* GUARD.

CATHERINE: He seems… lovely. There are obviously some cultural differences at play, that I will soon get used to and we will soon be as one.

ARCHIE: Aren't you gorgeously optimistic. I am Archbishop Samsa. I will perform the service. Marial will take care of your needs, a dress and jewellery have been picked out for you.

CATHERINE: Thank you.

ARCHIE: Welcome to Russia, Princess, we are servants of God and the Emperor.

CATHERINE: Of course I aim to be true to both.

ARCHIE: I now need to find out if you are intact.

CATHERINE: Perfectly fine, thanks for asking. A long journey I grant you, but I am excited by new life and so I feel quite, quite well.

ARCHIE: No, whole internally. That your interior wall has not been breached by another.

CATHERINE: Huh?

ARCHIE: Your sex.

CATHERINE: My what?

He points his crucifix at her crotch.

How dare you!? I am perfectly intact and that I would let you… disgusting… outrageous. I am a princess, an aristocrat, of noble birth and blood. A Catholic! How could you even think I would have allowed anyone to—?

ARCHIE: Well… you are French.

ARCHIE *steps toward her. Lights down.*

SCENE THREE

Catherine's quarters.

Catherine's servant, MARIAL, *pours water into a bowl.* CATHERINE *enters in nightgown.*

CATHERINE: Me, a married a woman.

MARIAL: Congratulations.

CATHERINE: Thank you.

MARIAL: Excuse me, Empress, you are ready for tonight? Would you like to talk about anything?

CATHERINE: I know what you are saying, and while I have not been with a man, my mother has explained everything.

MARIAL: She has?

CATHERINE: Yes, the man caresses you softly, pressing his lips to yours. Your breasts and skin awaken and shiver with a palpitating joy, between your legs quivers and moistens with longing, he enters you and you become one, your bodies meld, your souls mesh, as the sensation takes hold of you, you fall into a black sky filled with the shiniest of stars. You float for a time in ecstacy before waves of pleasure push and pull you back into your body. Your body ushers forth yelps and sometimes song, before he and you both explode within, and then you collapse together spent and unified. Then you lay together laughing softly, weeping occasionally with ecstatic joy and finally, he wraps his arms around you, whispers poetry softly into your ear and you fall into a delicious sleep.

> MARIAL *stares at her… starts to say something… then smiles.*

MARIAL: That's pretty much it.

> *Voices are heard approaching.* MARIAL *exits.* CATHERINE *readies herself.* PETER *is talking to a friend.*

PETER: [*offstage*] But he kept saying it is brilliant, let me bring the ducks to you, instead of having to find them I will call to them with my— [*He enters at this point.*] Just wait here a sec… Hello.

CATHERINE: My dear Peter.

PETER: [*to outside*] But then he does it, and sure enough ducks come from everywhere, but not four or five, like fifty…

GUY OUTSIDE: [*offstage*] It is hilarious.

> PETER *has unbuttoned himself.*

PETER: It was. Truly comical. Fucking ducks, hundred of them, we all just started…

He bends a dazed CATHERINE *over and enters her.*

We're running for cover, firing like crazy, ducks are dropping, people are screaming.

GUY OUTSIDE: [*offstage*] I would love to see it.

PETER: I will get him to do it again but this time we will… aaah… watch from the balcony. No danger to us. Whew. Have a pleasant evening, Empress. [*As he exits.*] So tell me what's going on in Kiev?

SCENE FOUR

Six months later.

CATHERINE *sits on the floor reading, a small stack of books beside her.*
PETER, ARCHIE, VELOMONTOV *and* ORLO, *a man in his thirties, enters.*

PETER: What are you doing in here?

CATHERINE: I am reading.

ARCHIE: A woman should not be alone. Unchaperoned. Where is your maid?

CATHERINE: I sent her out to find some arsenic for your tea.

ARCHIE: You have a sharp tongue.

PETER: [*sniggering*] Which normally I like in a woman.

He looks at them. They all laugh reluctantly with him.

But in this case…

VELOMONTOV: It is lovely to see you, Empress, the light hitting your face illuminating your radiance.

ORLO: Is that the new Voltaire? Is it good?

CATHERINE: Yes it—

PETER: We are to meet here.

CATHERINE: I am here. Reading.

PETER: The women are out on the lawn, they have a giant ball and are pushing it down the slope and chasing it.

CATHERINE: Then what happens?

PETER: It gets to the bottom and… I guess they do it again.

CATHERINE: What a perfect metaphor.

PETER: It looks hilarious, it looks fun, you could do with some fun. You're incredibly dull.

CATHERINE: I am happy here with my books.

PETER: Yes, but I am not and that is what matters. There are other rooms. Nine hundred and six of them.

CATHERINE: Then you will have no trouble finding another.

PETER: This is where we are to meet, though.

ARCHIE: You would do well to read your Bible.

CATHERINE: And you would do well to keep your fingers out of other people's business.

ARCHIE: I am God's servant.

CATHERINE: His right-hand man, so to speak. I do not like the Bible. I find it offers fools too many places to hide. It also seems badly written.

PETER: That's got to be blasphemy, doesn't it?

ARCHIE: It is God's word.

CATHERINE: It is the scratchings of ill-educated men from a thousand years past who smelt of hummus, lived in and believed the world flat. I can't take my lead from them. I prefer these men, or Shakespeare.

PETER: See, now you got her talking. And when I say talking I mean ranting.

ARCHIE: You are perilously close to blasphemy, Empress.

PETER: That's what I thought!

CATHERINE: If I were God that is who I would write through, these men with words of feeling and wit and depth and heart and love, who aspire for all of us to be complete with dignity, not funny little tales about an ark and lots of animals, or bushes that catch fire and start chatting, pages that call for the killing of infidels.

ARCHIE: Our war is just.

CATHERINE: And I'm sure they think the same, and when all the blood washes off the roads between here and there, which of you will be closer to your God?

PETER: You have a smart tongue, wife.

CATHERINE: And you a dumb one, husband, to go with your limp mind and bloodless heart.

ARCHIE: She has the devil in her.

CATHERINE: No, but I am in hell.

PETER: They have ribbons… the women on the lawn, in a variety of colours, they are running with them and they blow in the breeze, then I think they're having pink cake.

CATHERINE: I cannot go onto the lawn as that is where you shot my bear.

PETER: Still with the bear.

CATHERINE: You shot it!

PETER: As a joke, a lark, a jape.

CATHERINE: It was horrible.

PETER: Everyone laughed.

CATHERINE: You had a gun! They were scared you'd shoot them!

PETER: No, they had a sense of humour! Something you have yet to unpack from your baggage. You are the only person I have ever met who has not loved me. It's inconceivable to me. And says nothing good about you.

CATHERINE: If you had treated me with an ounce of kindness, I was ready with a heart full of love and sweetness.

Beat.

PETER: Um… You look really pretty. You done something to your eyes?

CATHERINE: Sobbed for six months.

PETER: Get out!

CATHERINE: They were blue and now they're a leached-out milky grey.

VELOMONTOV: Still pools so deep that man might dive in and happily die from the delight of swimming in them.

Beat.

ORLO: Perhaps the map room is free.

PETER: You should see this one when I fuck her, lying there, glassy-eyed, staring at me accusingly, reminds me of when once I shot a deer and I came upon it on its last breath, dead but still warm, I wondered what it would be like to fuck it, so I fucked it, and with her it's a lot like that.

CATHERINE: You are vile.

PETER: No, I am the Emperor! Okay, you three get out, the Empress and I need to speak.

CATHERINE: I will leave.

She goes to walk past him. He stops her, grasping her elbow.

PETER: Too late for that.

ORLO: The discussion about the new strategy is pressing your—

PETER: Did I say talk?! No, I said out. Which is different to talk! Isn't it?! Kate, you're well read, they're different, right.

ARCHIE, VELOMONTOV *and* ORLO *exit.*

Okay, I feel like you're unhappy with me.

CATHERINE: Don't mock me. My heart is breaking. I am lonely for my family, for France, for strawberries, sun, friends, ideas.

PETER: And I need my cock sucked.

CATHERINE: What?

PETER: We're sharing, right. Our needs. Well, I need my cock sucked.

CATHERINE: You are a pig.

PETER: France isn't going to happen. Family, your mother died, forgot to tell you, strawberries, I'll work on it. Friends, the court's full of women you can chat to.

CATHERINE: Gossiping morons waiting for the next affair or scandal.

PETER: You're so judgemental, you might want to look at that. You know your problem. You have no idea how lucky you are. There are soldiers dying.

CATHERINE: Because of you.

PETER: Serfs who're beaten daily.

CATHERINE: You could stop that. If you would just read some of these books. The ideas. We could rule as one…

PETER: I rule! You serve! God, is it that difficult? What happened to that happy little girl who gave me a twig?

CATHERINE: She died. I have tried, wanted to love you, tried to love you.

PETER: I am mostly kind to you. Do I beat you?

CATHERINE: I am a prisoner here and a slave and I feel the blows of your disdain daily.

PETER: But it's not the same as actual blows, is it?

CATHERINE: I—

He punches her in the stomach.

PETER: Don't really know? Now you do, compare and get back to me on it.

He sits in a chair. CATHERINE, *winded, lies on the floor.*

We've got problems, haven't we? My mother and father never acted like this. My mother was a saint! I'm glad she's not alive to see this. Not that I'm glad she's dead. I'm not. Never. Sometimes, once, but... no. Why are you? See what you're doing? Don't look at me like that. You are a disappointment to me as well. Still, there must be pleasure between a man and wife.

He starts undoing his pants.

CATHERINE: No. I will not!

PETER: I don't need a wife with a poisonous mouth and a dry cunny. I will shut you up at my pleasure and you will be happy. You will die here in content old age having given me hours of pleasure and service. [*Beat.*] You will come here, or I will come there. I do have a temper and some rage, you cannot cross me, especially not in front of others, or you will pay endlessly, and you will never win, you will just be in pain. It's up to you... On the other hand, the women have ribbons and a giant ball.

SCENE FIVE

Catherine's private quarters.

MARIAL *is pouring tea out of a samovar. She sets it on a table next to a chaise lounge.* CATHERINE *comes in and flops down face first on the chaise lounge.*

MARIAL: Would you like cake as well, Empress?

CATHERINE: No, I would like you to bring a large knife and find a blue vein and cut my wrists for me. Then you may take the afternoon off.

She holds her hands out. MARIAL *looks at her.*

MARIAL: I cannot.

CATHERINE: Then I will do it myself, but really what is the point of having servants if they will not do as you ask?

MARIAL: You are sad.

CATHERINE: Suicidal, it's different. If you want to steal some stuff before I go, feel free.

MARIAL: Madam...

CATHERINE: Do not try and talk me out of it, my mind is made up, I will leave now and God bless my soul.

MARIAL: I wasn't, I mean, can I really steal stuff? The silver inkwell?

CATHERINE: Sure, the silver inkwell. Maybe take some of the linen handkerchiefs for all the tears you'll obviously shed at my passing.

MARIAL: The Empress will have made her choice and I will be resolved with her that it was the right choice, for how could someone so smart and wise and book-readingly make the wrong choice.

CATHERINE: Clever. For a serf.

MARIAL: God made me a serf, it is the only thing that makes me feel he may not be infallible.

CATHERINE: Heretical too. I'm beginning to like you. Why do you speak French?

MARIAL: My mother was a whore...

CATHERINE: What is it with you people thinking we're all whores!?

MARIAL: Her price was higher if she could speak French. Although saying 'bonjour' with a mouth full of cock doesn't sound all that romantic, it upped the price a few roubles. Anyway, your knife.

CATHERINE: Your inkwell.

MARIAL: I appreciate it.

CATHERINE: There's no other way. I am a prisoner here.

MARIAL: Indeed.

CATHERINE: Married to an idiot.

MARIAL: It has never happened to a woman before.

CATHERINE: Yes, but to an Emperor, a madman! A killer!

MARIAL: He is one of a kind, it's true.

CATHERINE: I am doomed.

MARIAL: I will get a bucket for the blood.

CATHERINE: What am I to do? Live at someone else's whim?

MARIAL: God forbid, Empress. I will get the knife and bucket.

CATHERINE: You think I am some spoiled child, who has it so good, and should just shut up and eat her cake.

MARIAL: I don't have an opinion.

CATHERINE: Ever since I was a child I have felt like greatness was in store for me. A great love I felt. I felt marked out. Like God had spat me out and I landed on the earth in a brushed silk dress with diamonds in my ears. That he had put me here for a reason. A purpose.

MARIAL: Why did he make you a woman, then?

CATHERINE: For comedy, I guess. That idea, now it feels like some kind of delusion, and yet I felt it, Marial, in my being.

MARIAL: My mother once sucked Leo the First's cock.

CATHERINE: Interesting tangent.

MARIAL: During the coup against him.

CATHERINE: The coup?

MARIAL: They moved against him, he was killed. Burst into the room and grabbed him out of Mother's mouth. They left her, just a whore. They hung him.

CATHERINE: Really? Are there men here who are unhappy?

MARIAL: There are always men who are unhappy. How else would anything ever get done.

CATHERINE: Why do they not act?

MARIAL: They are cowards, they need a reason, a focus.

CATHERINE: Other than he is a nightmare?

MARIAL: Yes.

CATHERINE: I do not have any leeway, anything to offer, anything they want.

MARIAL: I have seen some of the men look at you, you have something they want.

CATHERINE: Oh. Enough to…

MARIAL: We're speaking of men, so yes, probably. Do you know how to seduce a man?

CATHERINE: I am French!

MARIAL: Of course. Though it is Russia, so... nothing too subtle.

CATHERINE: How about...? [*She lifts up her dress.*] Come and get it!

They both laugh.

I will seduce someone and we will kill him. I can't believe I just said those words.

MARIAL: They fell from your lips quite naturally. Empress.

SCENE SIX

Catherine's apartment. Later.

CATHERINE *waits, champagne on ice, taking various poses on the settee. Finally she takes up a leaning pose on the wall. Nerves overcome her and she suddenly goes over to the bucket which the champagne is in and vomits.* ORLO *enters at this point.*

ORLO: We are a long way from the sea.

CATHERINE: What?

ORLO: Mussels, right? You had the mussels last night. I never have them, we're a long way from the sea.

CATHERINE: I throw up every morning, it has nothing to do with mussels. It is the realisation I am still in Russia.

ORLO: Of course. My apologies.

CATHERINE: No... no, my dear Count Orlo, no apology is necessary, please come in. You are in. I see. I am glad you could come.

ORLO: It is a pleasure, I have been wanting to discuss Voltaire with you for some time. I have brought you a pamphlet by Diderot.

CATHERINE: Giving me gifts. Alone in my apartment. It is completely inappropriate, you know.

ORLO: Should we go to the garden? I didn't realise, it was... I'm sorry, it's my fault. I—

CATHERINE: It is thrilling to break the rules, is it not?

ORLO: I can't wait to confess and see Archie's face.

CATHERINE: You call the Archbishop Archie?

ORLO: I call him lots of things, that's the kindest one.

CATHERINE: You do not like him?

ORLO: He seems keen to fill heaven as fast as possible.

CATHERINE: Maybe he's on commission.

ORLO: Maybe he needs a woman.

CATHERINE: He put his fingers inside me.

ORLO: Oh. Okay. Well… that's not good, is it. Hmmm. Where, where where… are we?

CATHERINE: Let's not… talk of that. That's not why we're here. You have caught my eye.

ORLO: I am flattered. Shall we read?

CATHERINE: Is that what you want to do?

ORLO: Of course. Are you okay? You seem… something.

CATHERINE: Do I? Does it… stir you? Champagne?

They both look at the vomit in ice bucket.

ORLO: Um… thinking not.

CATHERINE: Oh… shit… of course. Um…

ORLO: I don't need anything. Thanks.

CATHERINE: Right. Good. Thanks. I mean… Really, you don't need anything? I guess not, but is there anything you… want?

ORLO: Oh my God! You're trying to seduce me!

CATHERINE: [*weakly*] Come and get it.

ORLO: I kind of suspected, You were being all breathy and repetitive. But then you did throw up, it was a little confusing.

CATHERINE: I'm new at it.

ORLO: I certainly would have sex with you. Certainly. Shall we do that? Or shall we read first?

CATHERINE: I am a failure. Utter failure.

ORLO: No you're not! Let's have sex! I'm very excited!

CATHERINE: No, but thanks. You're a sport.

ORLO: You're seducing me, though? I don't understand.

CATHERINE: What can I say, I'm complex.

ORLO: Oh God, this is, I am not well versed in the ways of women. I have in some way ruined things. I apologise.

Beat.

CATHERINE: You have not, Orlo.

ORLO: What is it then?

CATHERINE: I was hoping you'd be mad with desire for me and you'd help me kill Peter. A coup. I am unhappy. You wouldn't, would you? Kill him for me?

ORLO: I'd like to, anything to please, but right now is not a good time.

CATHERINE: Got a lot on?

ORLO: Why me anyway? I am not a soldier. I am… a bookish fellow.

CATHERINE: You are well liked, people trust you, Peter included, you network as well as anyone in the court, and yet you occasionally speak of Voltaire and Diderot, and when you do I see a light in you. You are close to the General, without whom no-one will move against Peter, which may be why you are close to him, I had hoped. They say you are like a son to him.

ORLO: I listen to his crap while smiling serenely, so yes, exactly like a son.

CATHERINE: So there you have it.

ORLO: Now that you say it, I am a strangely good choice for it. Isn't that odd.

CATHERINE: I hoped you believed in… something… in Russia.

ORLO: I do.

CATHERINE: And you think Peter is good for Russia?

ORLO: I think he is a disaster we may not recover from.

CATHERINE: And yet you will not act?

ORLO: I act all the time. As you say, I spread ideas. I talk. I believe in ideas, change the way people think you change the world, these seeds planted that will eventually root and flower and choke to death the superstition and fear and bloodthirsty ways of ours.

CATHERINE: And how long do you expect that to take?

ORLO: Two to five hundred years.

CATHERINE: You would not like to see it happen sooner, say while we still have our looks?

ORLO: It is what it is. These ideas will spread, you will see. In two hundred years we will not be ruled by these things, there will be light.

CATHERINE: I could slap you!

ORLO: What? Why?

CATHERINE: Because you have been given these gifts and you will not act! You have the capacity and you know you do, you know how you would engineer it, you have me to be the figurehead, you are a bloodless freak. There is nothing in your heart but air, all the blood is in your brain!

ORLO: Do not act as if you care about Russia! You just want someone to kill your husband.

CATHERINE: I promised myself a great love, that didn't work out, so be it. So now I have promised myself a great life.

ORLO: Everyone does that. Then they grow up. Realise there are parameters.

CATHERINE: And if not, construct them.

ORLO: I did not invent the monarchy, the feudal system, Christianity and smallpox.

CATHERINE: But you will not dismantle them.

ORLO: I do what I can. You married badly. I'm sorry, you made a mistake. Don't drag me and Russia into this.

CATHERINE: Russia and I are married to the same man, it is the same thing. You would not like to see a strong vibrant Russia alive with ideas and humane and progressive where people live with dignity and purpose in your lifetime?

ORLO: I would like to see it, and a green pig, and a talking turtle and a dog that cooks omelettes, but I feel I may have to die disappointed.

CATHERINE: Well, there's an aspiration. To die disappointed. Good luck with that, I suspect you'll make it.

ORLO: I have looked at the situation, at what I can achieve within reason.

CATHERINE: What is the point in believing in something if you will not act for it? I believe in reason but I believe only action and passion will achieve it. I will not live my life on the sidelines, some half-hearted coward!

ORLO: And how's that working out for you?

CATHERINE: Not so good.

ORLO: Maybe you could try my way.

CATHERINE: Don't you want to be consumed by something?

ORLO: Yes, but not Peter's executioner.

CATHERINE: I'd rather die than live some half-life wandering the halls whispering ideas. 'Oh sure, I'll have sex with you, Empress, gee that sounds really great.' You risk nothing. You make me sick.

ORLO: Well, there's a bucket right there. I'll be clear this time, you're not seducing me when you vomit.

CATHERINE: It was my luck to pick a eunuch.

ORLO: You would've confused a stallion! Treason is what we're discussing here, which could have us both with our stomachs slit open and him pouring baby rats into it before sewing us up. And don't think you are immune from that just because you are the Empress.

CATHERINE: I hate rats.

ORLO: Me too.

CATHERINE: What else do you hate?

ORLO: I hate the war. I hate that the streets are full of limbless men.

CATHERINE: Careful, Orlo, your voice raised an octave, you will have blood entering your left ventricle at any moment, maybe you should sit a little.

ORLO: You mock me. But I have had to hold myself from cutting their throats a hundred times. I love this country, I believe in ideas, I believe they are a virus that will spread through the world with light.

CATHERINE: What do you hold yourself back for? Isn't this your life?

ORLO: Yes, so I'd like to hang onto it.

CATHERINE: Why? You will leave a small dent in the carpets that will be swept away the day you die. A small man. A small dent. Some hot air. His name was Orlo.

ORLO: Fuck you!

CATHERINE: Stop it, you're running away with your crazy self.

ORLO: I am… you are… if we were to do this…

CATHERINE: … you would have to be a different man. A man who believed in a different country, who believed in action and not just ideas, a man who would join hands with me and try and make this country great, who would rule with love and fairness, but who knew they had to take power, it would not be given. A man who had been on fire all this time, but finally one day let himself take the lid off, and let the fire burn away the fear and leave him raw and ready to do what it took and to die if needs be in the process, but they would both die knowing they had lived as they should! You would have to be that man.

They stare at each other.

ORLO: Who would be in charge?

CATHERINE: I would be Empress, figurehead.

ORLO: Figurehead implies you are more symbolic and do as I and others would say.

CATHERINE: We will be needing a different word then.

SCENE SEVEN

The garden.

PETER *stands with a silver dish filled with strawberries. He speaks to someone out of sight.*

PETER: Just stay there. And quiet. I can hear you breathing.

VOICE: [*offstage*] Sir.

PETER: And now speaking!

CATHERINE *arrives.*

Catherine, thank you for coming. Have a strawberry, in fact have all of them.

CATHERINE: Thank you.

PETER: You ask, you get. You hear that. Okay. I wanted to apologise for the other day, that little… tiff we had.

CATHERINE: When you punched me?

PETER: Yeah, that day. See, here's what I think's happened. You've come in here with a very romantic notion of me and marriage and your life. A little naive I guess, not a criticism, it's actually a lovely attribute, and I was dumb not to realise it for what it was. You met me, and I am not a romantic man, kind of a practical chap, I like to have fun, larks and japes and weird sex, that's me, can't apologise for who I am, you don't want to ride that pony and I get that. I think I was angry because, no-one's ever not liked me...

CATHERINE: Or at least everyone's pretended to.

PETER: See, that's cruel, I mean really, I'm opening up to you here and you're like raining blows on my pink soft flesh.

CATHERINE: But not literal ones.

PETER: Tooosh.

CATHERINE: It's *touché*.

PETER: Really? Not tooosh.

CATHERINE: No. *Touché*.

PETER: See, that's great, how smart you are. I love that. My point is look, we're married, it is so, but we don't do it for each other.

CATHERINE: True.

PETER: On the other hand, accepting that truth might be liberating for us.

CATHERINE: I... I'm listening.

PETER: A nice change.

CATHERINE: Take the moment, then.

PETER: You have everything, finest of everything, carriages, homes, clothes, shoes, parties, servants, books, travel.

CATHERINE: Not love.

PETER: No, well I can't bring everything to the party. You will have to go find that for yourself. And I think you should.

CATHERINE: I don't understand.

PETER: A life without love, with someone you hate, makes you hate that someone more. I can't have it. So forget me and us, that carriage has sailed. Find yourself someone to love, live as Empress though, have all the advantages and none of the disadvantages. I want you to be happy. You're really a drag around the court. It reflects badly on me and makes me angry, then I start punching you, I wonder who I am. I was a jolly young chap, always have been, except when Mama was around I felt paralysed around her... someone should work out what goes on between mothers and sons, there'd be money in that.

CATHERINE: I dare say. I should take lovers?

PETER: Yes. You should find love. We should reach an accommodation. Because what's the alternative? I kill you. I don't want to be one of those guys who has to kill his wife. I just never imagined myself that way. I don't want to kill you. You're not a bad person.

CATHERINE: I could kill you. You are a bad person.

Beat. He starts laughing.

PETER: See, I like you, you're funny in a droll, despairing way. I couldn't take a lot of it, but occasionally it's refreshing. Would it be so bad?

CATHERINE: I don't know.

PETER: We have enough in common to get on.

CATHERINE: I don't think so.

PETER: We do. We're… both pretty.

She looks at him and laughs disbelievingly, but not unkindly.

I make you laugh. I found you a lover as well.

CATHERINE: You? Picked me a lover?

PETER: This was my criteria. The opposite of me. Here, have a bear.

A PAGE *walks a bear on stage. He tugs at its lead.*

CATHERINE: Oh my God.

PETER: Just in from Siberia. Sorry about the last one. It's a gesture.

CATHERINE: It is, thank you.

PETER: One thing. I'm still going to need an heir.

CATHERINE: We're going to have to—

PETER: Is it that unpleasant? Don't answer that. I don't want to think about that. The doctor could give you a sleeping draft. I could just come in, once every month or so, go hard, go fast, get in get out, you won't feel a thing I promise.

CATHERINE: Well, I didn't the other times.

He laughs, she laughs.

PETER: What do you say? Want to be happy?

The bear suddenly turns on his PAGE, *attacking him. They disappear offstage.*

CATHERINE: Stop! No!
PETER: Oh no. Stop.

He pulls his gun and fires a shot offstage. The bear growls and then falls. He and CATHERINE *look at each other.*

I'll get you another.

SCENE EIGHT

Catherine's quarters.

CATHERINE *and* ORLO *enter.*

ORLO: That went well.
CATHERINE: They seemed convinced. We are a good team.
ORLO: I give them reason and you... scare them.
CATHERINE: I do?
ORLO: Kind of. You hold a mirror up and say, 'Look at yourself. Is this who you really are?' When they cannot bear to look, you say, 'I believe it is the wrong reflection, there is a different one to be seen'.
CATHERINE: They will not shift to action without the General, though?
ORLO: They still fear defeat, with the General on board it will tip the balance. Others will swing in behind it just to be on the right side of it.
CATHERINE: How do we get him?
ORLO: I do not know, to approach him directly is to ask for a sliced throat. I will think on it.
CATHERINE: There was a lot of mention of... I thought bloodless coup when I first thought, except for Peter obviously.
ORLO: He has loyalists, guards who would die for him, and will have to.
CATHERINE: I feel a bit...
ORLO: Nauseous.
CATHERINE: Yes.
ORLO: I know.
CATHERINE: I shall put it out of my head.
ORLO: I heard he gave you a dead bear.

CATHERINE: He is a giving person.

ORLO: Mostly pain of course.

CATHERINE: As the bear would testify, although he did drop it with one shot.

ORLO: You sound impressed.

CATHERINE: Disgusted, but it made me think we should show him the same courtesy. I am also to have a love, he has chosen for me.

ORLO: He is absurd.

CATHERINE: Ridiculous.

ORLO: A fool.

CATHERINE: An idiot.

MARIAL: [*entering*] A monomaniacal deadshit.

CATHERINE: Marial!

MARIAL: Sorry.

CATHERINE: Don't be. I'm just impressed.

MARIAL: He is a Cock! A Shit. An Arse! A Ponce and a Nonce!

They laugh. HERMES *enters. They look up.*

CATHERINE: You just walk into my chambers, sir?

HERMES: I would have ridden but my horse has trouble with stairs.

PETER *enters.*

PETER: Empress, bookworm.

ORLO: Sir.

PETER: I have brought you a gift. I knew you were sad about the bear and it will take me a while to get a fresh one so…

HERMES *unrolls a rug on the floor. It is the skinned bear.*

CATHERINE: Oh, my God.

PETER: It is thoughtful of me, I agree. It will keep you company till the new one comes. But that's not all. This is Hermes, he is the rest of your gift. He is smart, reads books, recites sonnets, can hunt with the best, enjoys fine wines and offal, and apparently has a pretty big cock. I hope you like him. [*To* ORLO] Bookworm, I need to talk to you, about this road tax business.

ORLO: Certainly, sir.

PETER: Why are you here, anyway?

ORLO: Swapping books, sir.

PETER: God, you're a faggot. Let's go then.

He exits. CATHERINE *and* ORLO *huddle.*

CATHERINE: He is insane.

ORLO: And will be gone soon.

CATHERINE: How many will die?

ORLO: As few as possible.

PETER: [*offstage*] Am I being made to fucking wait!?

ORLO: We are together now.

He kisses her hand and exits. HERMES, *who brought the rug, is still there. She eyes him.*

CATHERINE: You may go.

HERMES: I'd rather not.

CATHERINE: I do not care. I said you may go. Do you really think I would want a man who would give himself to me at the Emperor's behest? Who could not come from his heart and decide for himself?

HERMES: Maybe I already did decide. Maybe the minute I walked in and laid eyes on you.

CATHERINE: Really?

HERMES: Maybe. Then again, I may just say that as he will possibly cut my throat if I don't please you. Then again, it's also possible that if I did please you, he could find himself unexpectedly and inexplicably jealous and cut my throat for pleasing you.

CATHERINE: You think he would be jealous?

HERMES: Of me. He is notoriously competitive, I found the head of a man who beat him at darts in the forest last week. Regardless, I would rather stay a while, so at least he thought it went well. If you don't mind. If you do, I cordially invite you to my execution and wish we had known each other better.

CATHERINE: Fine, you may sit a while. [*She goes to her writing table. She begins to write. She stops.*] You are fine just to sit?

HERMES: I am writing an opera in my head.

CATHERINE: I despise opera.

HERMES: It's not one of those dull ones full of fat Italian men chasing skinny waifs where everyone dies tragically in the end, this will have fat women chasing tiny men.

CATHERINE: Then what happens?

HERMES: They catch them and they fall in love. Then they die, it is an opera after all, but the men drown in the fat women's flesh, then the women die of heartbreak.

CATHERINE: So it is a comedy.

HERMES: I intend the audience to laugh so hard ribs will break, and cry so violently blood vessels in their eyes will burst.

CATHERINE: I expect it will not have a long run, then.

HERMES: You looked sad before, when you sat.

CATHERINE: Did I?

HERMES: Maybe you had some good news.

CATHERINE: You mean bad news.

HERMES: Things happen and we have the oddest responses to them, on learning of my father's death I could not stop laughing.

CATHERINE: You were not close.

HERMES: I loved him with every breath I had. But he had always said to me, 'Hermes, what will you do without me?' And I laughed when he died, because I thought of him watching me from above going, 'Here we go, now we'll see'. Which reminds me. [*Looking up*] Dad, here I am, that's the Empress, private quarters, lots of cushions, you know what I'm saying, doing fine. Watch and learn, old man.

CATHERINE: You are a strange one.

HERMES: Are you intrigued or repelled?

CATHERINE: You are striving for some effect.

HERMES: No, just curious. The truth is Peter will do with me as he sees fit and I really can't second guess how he will react. A man who talks of his mother so much cannot be trusted for stability.

CATHERINE: What did my husband say to you?

HERMES: He said I was to make you happy, said it was important to him, said if ever a woman needed a root, you were she.

CATHERINE: Oh, did he?

HERMES: Said if you showed any animation at all while we were doing it—emit a noise, stir a limb, puff a breath—he would give me a thousand roubles and have my cock bronzed and put on display in the Hermitage.

CATHERINE: And what did you say to that?

HERMES: I said, I thought the Hermitage could certainly use some new exhibits.

She laughs.

CATHERINE: And you told me this, why?

HERMES: Because you asked. And perhaps because I haven't been at court long and I didn't know and perhaps I was surprised…

CATHERINE: At what?

HERMES: What an asshole he is.

CATHERINE *laughs.*

CATHERINE: You could be hung for that.

HERMES: In this court you could be hung for anything. One cannot worry about that sort of thing.

CATHERINE: Who are you?

HERMES: Empress Catherine, I am Hermes. Just in from the West.

CATHERINE: How is it in the West?

HERMES: So beautiful, you could die from it.

CATHERINE: And yet you are here.

HERMES: I felt like living a little.

CATHERINE: Can you do that here? I hadn't noticed.

HERMES: You can do that anywhere. You just have to know how.

CATHERINE: Do you know how?

HERMES: It is all I know. It's a gift, but the money's not great.

CATHERINE: Speaking of which, shouldn't you have brought me a gift? Isn't that standard?

HERMES: I have indeed. I know my stuff.

He pulls an apricot from his pocket and hands it to her. She stares at it.

CATHERINE: You have made an error, it is not a gift. It is an apricot.

HERMES: I stole it from your orchard.

CATHERINE: It is still warm.

HERMES: When you eat it you should put it into your mouth, bite it once, tip your head back and let the juice run into your throat.

CATHERINE: I know how to eat an apricot.

HERMES: I will never underestimate you again.

She looks at him, then pops the apricot in her mouth and tips her head back.

CATHERINE: Oh, extraordinary, the juice runs in and pools at the…

They look at each other. Lights down.

SCENE NINE

Catherine's quarters.

ORLO *waits there.* MARIAL *is nearby.*

ORLO: Get a man drunk and naked in a sauna and the world is yours.

MARIAL: I'll be sure to remember that.

CATHERINE *enters.*

ORLO: Good morning. Great morning. Good Catherine. Great Catherine. You are well? You look radiant.

CATHERINE: I had a pleasant evening.

ORLO: As did I? Naked in the sauna with eight bottles of champagne and a fat pink naked General.

CATHERINE: I did not know you swung that way, Orlo… good for you… But really you could do better.

ORLO: Ah, my dear Catherine, I could not have done better, for I have found the key to our coup. The General is fond of you.

CATHERINE: Hence the drooling.

ORLO: Not fond, fond would not be enough, obsessed, plagued by fevered dreams of you on all fours.

CATHERINE: Oh, my God.

ORLO: He prays to his God, for relief from his lust, but relief will not come. He never speaks of personal things, just the war, strategy, policy, occasionally deer hunting, his love of his mother…

CATHERINE: Orlo!

ORLO: But so disturbed is he by his lust for you, he had to speak of it. We began speaking of you and flaccid to flagpole in thirty seconds, in his case not a long journey, but all the same. He is the key, with him the other generals follow.

CATHERINE: I will not fuck him.

ORLO: Oh.

CATHERINE: You assumed I would.

ORLO: People are prepared to die for this, you are seemingly fearless to me, I did not imagine. And you would fuck me, I figured. Besides, you will not have to, a whisper in his ear, a caress, a promise is all.

CATHERINE: You hope. His cock being thrust into you, not really a danger.

ORLO: Yes. I hope. And I trust in you, completely.

CATHERINE: I wasn't that great a seductress with you, remember?

ORLO: I am here.

CATHERINE: Yes.

ORLO: You have a way, you find a way, that is your greatness.

CATHERINE: Greatness? Okay, let's stop now. Maybe I cannot do this. I keep thinking of all the blood that will be spilt.

ORLO: People are excited, people feel like they may live now, even if they die.

CATHERINE: I have a big mouth and a pithy turn of phrase, people should take a moment to consider.

ORLO: I don't understand this sudden reticence.

CATHERINE: I just don't know whether I can seduce a man!

    HERMES *enters, no pants, just a shirt, etc.*

HERMES: Sorry, excuse me. I just have to look at you for a second. [*Beat.*] I was lying in bed and my head was filled with thoughts and images of you, visions, and you were so exquisite and beautiful it felt unreal, I had to come in and see if I had embellished it.

CATHERINE: And?

HERMES: A little, yeah.

    She laughs.

But still, exceptional. Now I will go. This seems serious and I try to stay away from that kind of thing.

>HERMES *exits. She watches him go, with a smile, then turns back.* ORLO*'s looking at her.*

CATHERINE: I know what you're thinking.

ORLO: Really? Does it have the word bitch in it?

CATHERINE: Orlo!

ORLO: You are in love…

CATHERINE: I am not!

ORLO: … and the rest of the world ceases to exist. My God, you're such a… woman!

CATHERINE: I am not in love. I had a pleasant night. I shared a warm apricot. That is all.

ORLO: Then we shall do this still?

CATHERINE: Of course we shall. You forget, it was my idea.

ORLO: [*satisfied*] Good day then.

>ORLO *exits.* CATHERINE *stands.* HERMES *comes in. He walks to her and spits a shower of rose petals out of his mouth. He kisses her. She kisses him back.*

HERMES: You are a taste I never want out of my mouth.

CATHERINE: Oh God!

HERMES: It does feel like we're in the middle of a religious experience, doesn't it?

CATHERINE: Last night was extraordinary. I felt things, my head was on your chest and your heart beat against my head, inside me in a way that was ridiculously… profound.

HERMES: Come.

CATHERINE: No. I… we… we must talk.

HERMES: Will we be needing our clothes?

CATHERINE: For the moment, yes.

>*She clasps her hands behind her back and paces.*

HERMES: I see. It is a serious talk involving clasped hands and pacing.

CATHERINE: Russia is in a mess, the ground thick with suffering and chaos, and here are we chattering like empty-headed birds and fornicating like dumb pigs.

HERMES: I would have said fine horses, but still.

CATHERINE: Everything is not a joke. Do you not care?

HERMES: I care. It is a corrupt, redundant, vicious place.

CATHERINE: Would you do something if you could? To change things. The politics of the country?

HERMES: It is not my job, it is for someone else, I am to live and love.

CATHERINE: More party animal than political animal.

HERMES: A cow doesn't give eggs.

CATHERINE: Do you not wish to do something about it?

HERMES: Complain to Peter. Maybe I will. And he will say, 'I did not realise. Thanks for the heads-up.' I was lucky to be born a minor aristocrat. But it is a tiny place I was given to live in. The challenge is to live in it. The joy is that I have found you to live in it with. And that expands my universe beyond these walls.

CATHERINE: You… just don't touch me while we talk.

HERMES: Why?

CATHERINE: It rearranges me.

HERMES: Me too.

CATHERINE: We cannot just lie around naked eating fruit and each other!

HERMES: I realised early on that dwelling on the stupidity of the way things are will serve no purpose other than to make me miserable and frustrated and I refuse to live like that. We were lucky enough to be trapped in Russia's slightly more pleasant halls, my challenge is to create and taste all that is glorious within it. It is my revenge.

CATHERINE: So your happiness is a political stand?

HERMES: Indeed it is. And I will not resile from it. Shall we have champagne?

CATHERINE: I do not know whether I admire it or despise it.

HERMES: Neither do I, so I suggest you do neither, merely enjoy me. Maybe lick me a little if you feel like it.

CATHERINE: You are incorrigible.

HERMES: And you are lovely and I am in love with you.

CATHERINE: Why would you say that to me?!

HERMES: Because it is true.

CATHERINE: It is ridiculous. We just met.

HERMES: We did. And it was like I had been waiting to meet you all my life. And you?

CATHERINE: But there are bigger things than us.

HERMES: That is exactly how it feels. Like something bigger is at work. I will flow with it. It leads to you.

CATHERINE: Hermes, stop!

> *Beat.*

HERMES: On our estate there is a wonderful field of wheat that my father and I would walk through and I would run my hands across the top of the stalks and feel the wind run through them. When I was twelve the war edged its way toward us and suddenly men appeared in the field. A skirmish broke out and the whole field was lost in blue smoke, with shapes like ghosts shifting amid it, then the fighting stopped, the smoke cleared, the field was dotted with bodies, the wheat flat and slick with blood. Then the bodies were interred, the men moved on, rain came and washed the blood away, we replanted and the wheat grew back and my father and I walked through the field again, and he asked me, 'Who won?'

CATHERINE: So it does not matter?

HERMES: We will all be dust. I will be happy dust. Is it wrong? To find happiness, love?

CATHERINE: No, it is not. I have waited for it my whole life.

HERMES: And here it is.

> *He puts his hand out to her.*

SCENE TEN

The lawns.

A polo match is in progress. PETER *prowls the sideline.* VELOMONTOV, ORLO, ARCHIE, CATHERINE *and* HERMES *are all present.*

PETER: Come on! Hit it!

ARCHIE: Terrible shot. Idiot.

PETER: Entertain me!

VELOMONTOV: I believe the soldiers will win.

PETER: Which will make it different from the war, hey fatso!

They wander away. CATHERINE *and* ORLO *are left alone.*

ORLO: Find a moment alone with the General and then you may—

CATHERINE: No.

ORLO: What?

CATHERINE: I can't do it. I mean, when you boil it down all I really wanted was to kill my husband. And if I was a girl from the villages that wouldn't be a problem. But all this, blood in the halls, bodies in the courtyard. Not to mention I do this, then I'm Empress. It's crazy. I have no qualifications. You know that.

ORLO: You are brilliant.

CATHERINE: Nice of you to say. But what have I ever done, pretty good breeding, lucky break there, read a few books, can string a few words together after a bucket of sherry, but you know… what if I'm no good?

ORLO: Will you skin people alive?

CATHERINE: No!

ORLO: Then you will be a vast improvement.

CATHERINE: This is what I think happened, I am this spoiled child who wanted to be Empress, to be loved, I came and was shocked and angry and felt for a moment to make someone pay. Out of rage.

ORLO: I saw more than that. I saw someone who sensed something in themselves. As do the others, which is why they agreed.

CATHERINE: When we die is it going to matter what we did? Or is it going to matter how we felt? That we were happy, and I am that, now. I lay in bed last night and asked myself who am I to want more. I have everything.

ORLO: And that is now the purpose of life, is it? To have everything.

CATHERINE: To have enough, to feel content.

ORLO: You can still have him and do it, it will be better, you will then be free.

CATHERINE: We could die if he finds out! Do you want that? You had a perfectly good life before I came and—

ORLO: You held a mirror up, and said look, and I did not like what I saw.

CATHERINE: I was wrong.

ORLO: I am a fool.

CATHERINE: You are not. I did you a disservice. You were happy with your books and your whispering.

ORLO: And you tore open something new and I will not put it back!

CATHERINE: We could die, we could lose, we could be absolute rubbish. Are you mad? You are a bookworm and I am a spoiled princess.

ORLO: So you are scared.

CATHERINE: Yes.

ORLO: As am I. Of failing.

CATHERINE: I am scared of succeeding. Of what it will take to succeed. And now I do not know the point of it.

ORLO: Or hope to forget it.

CATHERINE: We can still achieve things, Peter and I have achieved this peace, with it he will listen, already to you, but to me as well. We will influence, you and I are a powerful team, we have shown that.

ORLO: So you are going to be like him, your beau. I bet he is happy.

CATHERINE: He seems so. Is it a crime?

ORLO: Sometimes.

CATHERINE: You do not know him.

ORLO: Oh, I know him, he is one of those guys who floats through life and it's all fine wines and fig flans and pussy and pig shooting. Happy as a blind man in a slaughterhouse.

CATHERINE: Maybe you are simply jealous.

ORLO: That'd be easy for you, wouldn't it.

CATHERINE: It would make sense, you are a bookish little man and I am as fine a filly or fawn to parade these greasy halls in centuries. You probably only agreed to this to try and get inside my…

ORLO: Cunt.

CATHERINE: I was looking for something more... flowery, but yes. Exactly.

ORLO: I was not using it as an anatomical term. More an apposite description of how I feel about you right now. [*He goes to leave.*] This is why I love books, they never disappoint me.

CATHERINE: You will be safer, happier.

ORLO: No, I won't because now I am doomed.

CATHERINE: Why?

ORLO: Because I have felt what I could be. As have you, and so there is no escape for either of us.

He exits. HERMES *approaches.*

HERMES: Fig flan?

CATHERINE: I don't think so.

HERMES: You must, it is extraordinary.

CATHERINE: I will—

He shoves some in her mouth.

Oh my God, it is!

SCENE ELEVEN

Dinner. A table is set up.

PETER, VELOMONTOV *and* ARCHIE *sit talking.*

PETER: So I said... really? How fowl is fowl when you are already a chicken?

They laugh politely. CATHERINE *and* HERMES *enter.*

So don't you look radiant, wife?

CATHERINE: Thank you.

HERMES: Emperor.

PETER: Hermes. My wife looks happy, is she happy?

CATHERINE: I am.

PETER: Really? How happy? Extraordinarily so, screaming his name happy, or just, it'll do?

CATHERINE: Let's go with, it'll do. Don't you look… something.

PETER: It's a Kaminsky.

CATHERINE: What's that?

PETER: Ellen Kaminsky, she's a blind woman with the bony hands in the west wing.

CATHERINE: Oh I—

PETER: Excellent seamstress, her work during the ball season was extraordinary.

HERMES: Very slick indeed.

PETER: Excellent. Join us. Goose cooked in blueberries with fondant potatoes and caviar and vodka shooters on the side. Join me at the head of the table, my Queen.

CATHERINE: Of course.

> ORLO *enters.*

PETER: Orlo, where the fuck have you been? Head in a book or a woman?

ORLO: A book.

PETER: Disappointing. Sit, sit.

> CATHERINE *passes* VELOMONTOV.

VELOMONTOV: Empress, you look as if you fell from heaven.

CATHERINE: If I did my aim was bad.

> *She sits as they all do.* PETER *takes her hand.*

PETER: Archie, ever eaten goose like this?

ARCHIE: Never.

PETER: You're damn right never, these are Odessa forest geese.

ARCHIE: A gift from God.

PETER: Ever eaten pussy, Archie?

ARCHIE: No, I have taken vows.

PETER: So have I, eat as much as I can. Minute you feel the need let me know. I am in an expansive mood tonight, surrounded by you all. I spent the afternoon inspecting the heads of all these infidels brought back from the front. The look frozen on a man's face the instant he dies… why it is… really quite comical.

ORLO: May we speak of smallpox, Emperor?

PETER: Yeah, let's with mouthfuls of duck and blueberries, that'd be perfect. Next book you read, make it one on etiquette, Orlo. Anyway, lots of the heads still had their eyes in, and I… it was pretty funny. General, tell the rest, I'm the central character and it is an amusing anecdote featuring my gift for whimsy.

VELOMONTOV: You pretended you were in a bar and would then suddenly turn your gaze on one of the heads and…

PETER: I'd go, 'What are you looking at?!' Then I'd run at them and poke their eyes out. Oh, it was grand, did we laugh, Velomontov?

VELOMONTOV: Indeed, sir. If only we had all been there.

CATHERINE: The telling is ample, General.

PETER: Doesn't do it justice. Hey, there's more heads left. We could bring some up during dessert and I could do the whole thing again.

ORLO: They say a Scottish doctor has cured it, has a vaccine for it at the least. Smallpox.

ARCHIE: I have heard this but I do not believe it.

CATHERINE: Is it true?

ORLO: They say it is.

ARCHIE: I doubt it.

CATHERINE: Why is that?

ARCHIE: God does not work through Presbyterians.

CATHERINE: We should bring him here, Emperor, stop this plague.

PETER: Eat your goose, my duck.

CATHERINE: The people would love you.

PETER: They already love me.

CATHERINE: You would go down in history.

PETER: I am Emperor of Russia, that's a given.

ARCHIE: We should wait and see.

ORLO: Not enough piles of bodies dotting the kingdom yet, Archie.

ARCHIE: God takes who he takes.

ORLO: If only he would choose more wisely.

ARCHIE: You have discovered some venom of late, Orlo. Maybe you need confession.

ORLO: I will confess when I see a man of God in the halls.

PETER: I love it when these two go at each other, it is hilarious.

CATHERINE: What I think is—

> PETER *looks at her.*

If I may?

PETER: Of course, I love people who have no business in the affairs of state giving their opinions.

CATHERINE: Excellent, thank you—

PETER: I was being… someone?

VELOMONTOV: Facetious.

PETER: Yes!

CATHERINE: I did not read it so. I believe that with the war against the infidels sucking men into the earth as fast as we can send them—

VELOMONTOV: The new push will change—

PETER: Shut the fuck up, fatty! The Empress is talking.

VELOMONTOV: Of course, I am sorry.

PETER: Go on, darling. [*To* VELOMONTOV] Cunt!

CATHERINE: I think it would be worth trying the vaccine. In the interests of strengthening our army against the infidel. The vaccine will save many lives. If the war was paused while we rebuilt, we used the army to distribute the vaccine, it would take say a year, then we would be ready to finally crush them.

PETER: Lives we could then throw at the infidel! I love it. Nice. Thanks. Eat your goose.

ARCHIE: A year?

PETER: Hmmm. They are kicking our coits in. So Archie, save 'em so they can die for God, it's a thought.

ARCHIE: If only it were so simple, Emperor. I—

PETER: This better be short… is something moving in my goose? No no, my leg just jiggling the table.

ORLO: It is simple. We cannot stand by knowing we can cure this thing, and not do it, it is barbaric!

PETER: Orlo! No! Archie! Go!

ARCHIE: While I am moved by how the Empress suddenly cares for the war with the infidel. I believe our war with them to be the last war. The end of Days is upon us. The plague of the pox is part of the signs of it. When it is done, God will reveal himself, we are players in his final act, there is no need to meddle with his desires. We will prevail against them.

ORLO: [*to* ARCHIE] You are an apocalyptic deadshit.

PETER: Apocalyptic deadshit! Someone write that down, I don't know what it means but it sounds abusive.

CATHERINE: How do we know that? They're kicking our quoits in at the moment I believe.

ARCHIE: We will prevail because we are we and they are they.

PETER: And that's how it is with a hey hey hey. Why must I rhyme all the time?

HERMES: Because you are a poet though you did not know it.

PETER: And you are a wit who does access my wife's clit.

HERMES: With your permission and only for a moment.

PETER: My dear sir, you do not have to disown it.

HERMES: She is a remarkable treasure. I am honoured to be at her pleasure, but she is your wife, which I do not forget.

PETER: And you value your life, hence the rhyme, I bet.

HERMES: Emperor.

PETER: Rich, Hermes, rich. Have a shooter with me.

PETER & HERMES: [*together*] Huzzah!

PETER: So let's all go look at my heads?

CATHERINE: And the smallpox vaccine?

PETER: As Archie said. We must go with God.

CATHERINE: It is a mistake. And a heinous sinful act.

PETER: Whatever it is, it is at least two things, done as I say it will be, and none of your concern.

ORLO: Sir, if I may speak.

PETER: If you do, the third course will be your tongue. With a lovely salsa verde. I once had one in Venice and it was a revelation. We will stay the course we have set. The vaccine can wait, if it is real, in due course God will give us a sign. Okay, it seems dumb to bring the heads up here. Let's go to the heads. They will bring us dessert there and we will eat it under their beady gaze.

He leaves, they all follow. CATHERINE *sits.* HERMES *pulls her chair out.*

HERMES: I was thinking maybe tomorrow we should go down to that little cake shop Bonomie told me about, the brioche light as air, they fleck it with raspberries, then maybe we could look at shops, look... an ugly word, I know... browse, it has a sense of movement. Look I invented a word. Huzzah. Then there is a Molière on at the Pictu, a hilarious tale apparently.

CATHERINE: Shut the fuck up, you gibbering fop! Cake and raspberries and browse, here's a word I made up, castrate!

HERMES: Hang on, are you angry?

CATHERINE: That is not funny. Nor is your rhyming couplet with that sociopath.

HERMES: You mean your husband? I was playing the game, as were you.

CATHERINE: I was trying to get him to do something.

HERMES: So was I. Not kill me.

He goes to exit.

CATHERINE: Hermes. I am sorry. I am not myself. How can you bear it?

HERMES: What choice do I have?

CATHERINE: You could flee the court.

HERMES: I love you. You know in cards the bad players are the ones who do not play the hand they are dealt. They force a hand they do not have. They bluff and are mostly crushed, or they wait for God to deal them the card that will release them. This card almost never comes and they go broke buying cards to get it. I am a good card player, Catherine. And I will not throw in my hand because I didn't get all the right ones.

CATHERINE: I think I got a different hand.

HERMES: So play it.

SCENE TWELVE

Catherine's quarters.

VELOMONTOV *waits.* MARIAL *comes in from the other entrance.*

MARIAL: She will be with you soon. She is praying.

VELOMONTOV: Of course.

MARIAL: Has been for hours. I will have to apply cream to her knees again, she is devout.

VELOMONTOV: She has the glow of a saint.

MARIAL: Indeed. Sometimes we do not even light the candles the glow is that bright.

VELOMONTOV: I could not believe her summons, I had… dreamed I had… prayed, no, no, lust is not something one prays for.

MARIAL: It is just something one hopes for.

VELOMONTOV: I am not speaking to you.

MARIAL: Nor I to you, General.

> *He breathes into his hand and smells it.*

VELOMONTOV: Come here, girl.

> *He breathes in her face.*

How does it smell?

MARIAL: Like a fish that died around the time of my birth.

> CATHERINE *enters.* MARIAL *exits.*

VELOMONTOV: My dear Empress.

CATHERINE: I'm sorry to call you from your work, General, you have such weight on your shoulders, but I have a dilemma and the first time I saw you I sensed immediately your goodness and holiness. No, no, my mother always said to me, 'Catherine, you are… really good at sensing holiness and goodness'. And that's what I did. With you.

VELOMONTOV: I'm flattered.

CATHERINE: And perspiring.

VELOMONTOV: I'm sorry.

CATHERINE: Don't be, it's just a little distracting. Maybe you need a hand towel.

VELOMONTOV: I feel a flame from the inside that—

CATHERINE: Makes you leak, I understand. What do you think of Peter?

VELOMONTOV: He is the Emperor. I serve with loyalty and devotion.

CATHERINE: He seems to call you fatso and cunt a lot.

VELOMONTOV: The burdens of office are heavy upon him, he blows steam sometimes. I regard them as terms of endearment.

CATHERINE: A ridiculous rationalisation. You are a fool and a coward, I have made a mistake, you may leave.

VELOMONTOV: Empress, no, I—

CATHERINE: Thanks for your time, good luck with future projects.

VELOMONTOV: It is true they are harsh attacks.

CATHERINE: And how do you feel about that?

VELOMONTOV: I… it really hurts. Some nights I lay in bed and feel tiny tears on my cheeks.

CATHERINE: A big man like you weeping tiny tears, what a… embarrassing image.

VELOMONTOV: I have revealed myself to you, my heart, do not spurn me…

CATHERINE: Fuck off and don't tell me what to do. You are the first thing my husband has been right about, you are a fat cowardly blubbering cunt. As such I will not be needing you as I hoped.

VELOMONTOV: Your mouth.

CATHERINE: Could be your best friend or your worst enemy, could have a soft wet tongue in it, or could have a hard gob of spit for your teary little eyes.

VELOMONTOV: You are a cruel—

CATHERINE: God gives me the Devil's words to do God's work.

VELOMONTOV: I do not understand.

CATHERINE: You are dim, that is why.

VELOMONTOV: I am confused.

CATHERINE: Oh, General, is that a salty droplet quivering on your eyelid?

VELOMONTOV: Enough! I will not be subject to this… this…

CATHERINE: Abuse, is the word you seek. How does this happen to someone? The great irony being you are a soldier.

VELOMONTOV: Why is that an irony?

CATHERINE: Because it is synonymous with courage. And yet look at you.

VELOMONTOV: You will stop this! I am a man and I will be treated as such!

CATHERINE: Maybe when you act as such.

VELOMONTOV: I will do as you wish.

He comes toward her suddenly, pushing her to the ground. Holding her down, he starts to unbutton his pants.

CATHERINE: No!

VELOMONTOV: I understand, darling Catherine, you are afraid to give me your body, to ask for what you wish, so you will inflame me till I take you. I will give you what you wish.

CATHERINE: Oh fuck.

VELOMONTOV: I will, my darling, I will.

CATHERINE: No!

VELOMONTOV: When will they invent pants with fewer buttons!

CATHERINE: It is not that I inflame you for. It is to unprise you from your cowardice.

VELOMONTOV: And I will unprise, unveil and unleash momentarily. Three to go.

CATHERINE: It is God who calls me to this, in my dreams. And… and he says he sends you carnal dreams of me, is this true?

VELOMONTOV: I did not attribute them to God. But they plague me, I am sick with lust. Which has only one cure.

CATHERINE: It is not a sickness, he has bound us together for a reason. A purpose, this is no quick slick hit against a hallway wall like other court animals.

VELOMONTOV: It isn't?

CATHERINE: It is an exalted thing, this blaze of passion and righteousness he has set within us is to burn away our cowardice and set us on our course.

VELOMONTOV: And it is not the quick slick thing?

CATHERINE: I will show you something. Let me up.

He does so. She lifts her dress up and shows him her inner thigh.

VELOMONTOV: Oh dear God.

CATHERINE: Focus, Velementov. What do you see?

VELOMONTOV: A birthmark.

CATHERINE: No, it appeared six days ago on my flesh.

VELOMONTOV: The whiff of …

CATHERINE: Look at the shape.

VELOMONTOV: It is… it is Russia.

CATHERINE: He sends us a sign.

VELOMONTOV: To what end?

CATHERINE: To Peter's end of course.

VELOMONTOV: And then… we rule together.

CATHERINE: Something like that, yes.

VELOMONTOV: Of course.

CATHERINE: So we will do this, will we not?

VELOMONTOV: Yes. He has given us to each other. It makes sense the lust I felt, unlike me to feel so much, so uncontrolled, even flagellation could not sustain me. We should consummate our union. In his name.

CATHERINE: Button up, tiger. We are not to, until we have paid our dues to him. To Russia. Only then will I lay out naked and luminous, wet and pliant, with legs that stretch all the way to St Petersburg.

VELOMONTOV: I am starting to sweat again.

CATHERINE: Go to Orlo and speak of this to him.

VELOMONTOV: I will.

He suddenly embraces and gropes her.

CATHERINE: Enough. Go forth and let us do his work.

VELOMONTOV: I will. But one whiff to carry me.

He gets on his knees, She lifts her skirt and flaps it. He makes some weird wolf sound.

You have released something in me.

He goes.

CATHERINE: I think it is called insanity.

MARIAL *enters, wash bowl and cloth in hand.*

MARIAL: Did it work?

CATHERINE: I think so.

> *She lifts her skirt,* MARIAL *starts washing off the birthmark.*

All I can say is thank God for buttons.

MARIAL: They ever invent something easier, we're all in a lot of trouble.

SCENE THIRTEEN

Catherine's quarters.

CATHERINE *and* HERMES *gambol about.*

HERMES: You are in high spirits today.

CATHERINE: I believe I am. Here's a topic. You and me and the future.

HERMES: I like the sound of that.

CATHERINE: What about children?

HERMES: Never liked them, they're small and tend to get drunk too fast to be good companions.

CATHERINE: Would you have them with me?

HERMES: I don't think Peter would be pleased. But I will risk it and begin at once.

> *He starts to scurry under her dress. She laughs.* MARIAL *enters.*

MARIAL: Peter approaches.

> HERMES *scurries under her dress completely.*

CATHERINE: What are you—?

> PETER *enters.*

PETER: My dear wife.

CATHERINE: Hello. How are you?

PETER: To be honest, a little troubled. There is talk of talk.

CATHERINE: There is?

PETER: A possible coup. Fuckers, plotting against me. Me? Who've been nothing but kind… You try to be good to people and… Anyway, fuckers are going to be wearing their livers for hats when I get done.

CATHERINE: Do you know who?

PETER: Orlo and the General are looking into it.

CATHERINE: Good.

PETER: Anyway, just wanted to let you know. I doubt they'll come for you. Since it is your coup, that would seem disorganised.

CATHERINE: I don't know what you're—

PETER: Just testing. I have given Hermes two guards, they go with him everywhere, except when he is with you.

CATHERINE: I noticed that. Thank you for protecting him.

PETER: If a move against me is made, screams are heard, people are running in hallways their clothes sprayed with blood, or even just a vague certainty of moves afoot, they will cut his throat to the hard part at the back of his neck.

CATHERINE: What?

PETER: The cunt's dead.

CATHERINE: I…

PETER: You what? Do not wish that to happen? I imagined you wouldn't. We have engineered a suitable arrangement I thought.

CATHERINE: Do not.

PETER: Do not, yourself! I will leave you now, you have things to do. We should talk about children sometime.

He exits. She is left standing there. HERMES *backs out of there.*

HERMES: Damn, can't hear a thing under there. You jammed your legs together so hard my ears hurt. Ow.

She stares at him.

How is he?

CATHERINE: Mad.

HERMES: No change, then. Champagne.

She stares at him while he gets the bottle and pours.

CATHERINE: You know what I love about you?

HERMES: I'm handsome, witty and can make a noise exactly like a chicken caught in a fence?

CATHERINE: You always make me smile. No, I love that you have lived.

HERMES: I pride myself on it. I like to think if I died tomorrow I would be happy.

CATHERINE: I like to think that to.

Beat.

HERMES: Catherine?

CATHERINE: They are not guards. They are not protecting you. You are their hostage.

HERMES: They're going to kill me?

CATHERINE: Unless I stop the coup against Peter.

HERMES: There's a coup? Where have I been?

CATHERINE: Enjoying your life.

HERMES: You knew this?

CATHERINE: Yes.

HERMES: Wow.

CATHERINE: Wow?

HERMES: I don't know what it means, it just came out. Wow.

CATHERINE: I think it is right.

HERMES: So you have to stop the coup. Will it be hard? Do you know who's behind it?

CATHERINE: I am behind it.

HERMES: Whew. Wow. That had me worried, tense moment, need a drink, look at the hairs on my arms, and my heart. Wow. There I go again. Let's have a drink. [*He turns, grabs the glasses, and looks at her.*] Why are you crying? It's fine, you said yourself. You just—

CATHERINE: Kiss me.

HERMES: Catherine. No.

CATHERINE: I—

HERMES: You should think about what you're going to say next, about what sort of person you are, about how happy we are, that you love me, and I you! You should not speak about these things, but just think.

CATHERINE: I do love you. And I am sorry.

Beat. He looks at her, steps forward and kisses her.

HERMES: I will haunt you.
CATHERINE: Promise it.

SCENE FOURTEEN

Peter's study.

PETER *sits surrounded by severed heads. He has a head in front of him. And is feeding it.*

PETER: Come on, Ibrahim, have some.

ORLO *stands, a book in hand.*

Hello, bookworm, look I'm feeding them pork.
ORLO: Witty.
PETER: Isn't it? Because they're not allowed to eat it so—
ORLO: I get it. You know I have spoken to you of Voltaire.
PETER: I napped through several such lectures.
ORLO: What would it take to get it into your head, I asked myself? Then it came to me.

He smashes the book across PETER's *head.* PETER *goes down.* ORLO *drops the book and pulls a knife.*

SCENE FIFTEEN

HERMES *is walking. He suddenly stops, staring at something.*

HERMES: We could just go to a bar and forget the whole thing, boys. No? Okay. [*He looks up.*] Hey, Dad, I'm coming early.

SCENE SIXTEEN

CATHERINE *waits, screams are heard.* MARIAL *looks at her.* VELOMONTOV *enters.*

VELOMONTOV: My dear Empress. It is done.
CATHERINE: You are sure.

VELOMONTOV: I am sure. God has triumphed. We have triumphed.

CATHERINE: Marial, we will need champagne.

> *He comes toward her. She picks up a knife and stabs him in the gut. He topples to the ground.*

One glass.

SCENE SEVENTEEN

CATHERINE *sits on the floor, her glass of champagne beside her.* ORLO *stands there. He eyes* VELOMONTOV.

ORLO: The General?

CATHERINE: Does not look well. I agree.

ORLO: Anything to do with the knife in his gut?

CATHERINE: It can't be helping the bleeding, that's for sure. I saw him coming towards me, perspiring, arms outstretched, and I realised no-one sticks things in me I don't want stuck in me.

ORLO: A polite refusal?

CATHERINE: Was an option I chose to ignore. Is it a problem?

ORLO: We will say… Peter's men killed him. Peter is dead.

CATHERINE: And… Hermes?

ORLO: Yes. They found his body in the orchard.

> *She cracks out a sob for a second, then swallows it.*

I'm sorry.

> *She composes herself and raises a glass.*

CATHERINE: *Salut.*

ORLO: *Salut.* We will do great things.

CATHERINE: We will. Considering what it cost.

ORLO: I got you something.

> *He gives her a box. She looks inside.*

CATHERINE: Fingers!

ORLO: Archie's.

CATHERINE: Thank you. Shall we begin? I will talk and you will write down what I say and then it will happen.

ORLO: Politics is not so—Let me get a quill.

He gets up to get it. CATHERINE *stands.*

CATHERINE: The rich should be kind to the poor. The vaccine will be distributed. One man does not own another.

Fade out.

END OF ACT ONE

ACT TWO

SCENE EIGHTEEN

Thirty years later.

CATHERINE, *now in her early fifties, is having sex. She is astride* PLIMPTOV, *a young handsome banker in his forties.*

PLIMPTOV: Oh, Empress, how sweet you are, the nape of your neck, the scent of your—

    She stops and throws a look at him.

CATHERINE: I'm just wondering why you think it's okay to talk?

PLIMPTOV: I am filled with ardour for you, poetry fills my veins while you are astride me.

CATHERINE: It will not do. I have mentioned it before.

PLIMPTOV: But I love you.

CATHERINE: Say it again, your eyes are coming out. You are a fool, which I do not mind as you are aesthetically and functionally pleasing to me. You are however a loud fool, and that I despise.

PLIMPTOV: I feel a song when our eyes meet, I feel—

CATHERINE: You are one of my treasurers and it worries me this can happen to you, how safe is my money when some girl can turn your head this easily?

PLIMPTOV: No-one turns my head but you, you turn it three hundred and sixty degrees.

CATHERINE: I am certainly thinking of doing just that.

PLIMPTOV: I believe we could love each other, marry, and that every moment would be joyous and bliss.

CATHERINE: You are a preposterous little man. I have half a mind to drown you.

PLIMPTOV: I am not afraid of you as the others. I, George Plimptov, are not afraid, I feel you love me, dumpling.

CATHERINE: Dumpling? I will kill you, your parents, your wife and child, your horses, your dogs, your crops, your will to live, and then I will drink a cup of tea and have forgotten you before I finish it.

MARIAL *enters. She checks herself a little.*

CATHERINE: Yes, Marial.

MARIAL: Orlo is here.

CATHERINE: Oh God.

PLIMPTOV: It's good?

CATHERINE: Shut up!

MARIAL: Is it a bad time?

CATHERINE *looks at her.*

Right. He says it's urgent. A matter of the empire falling, of life and death, heaven and earth.

CATHERINE: He said that. What was his manner?

MARIAL: More amused than you would think, that being the situation.

CATHERINE: He means to interrupt me, it his idea of a joke. Send him in.

PLIMPTOV: Should I—?

CATHERINE: I'm assuming that noise I just heard wasn't you.

ORLO *enters.*

Oh, Orlo, how good to see you.

ORLO: Empress.

CATHERINE: You know Plimptov.

ORLO: I did not recognise him from this angle.

CATHERINE: I am training him in the pleasures of silence.

ORLO: You are a kind and generous woman.

CATHERINE: So I… Oooh… I hear the Empire falls by dinner.

ORLO: There are urgent matters before us.

CATHERINE: Of course. Plimptov, you may go.

She gets off him. He assembles himself and bows to ORLO.

ORLO: Plimptov.

PLIMPTOV: Orlo. Empress, you have my heart.

CATHERINE: We have discussed which parts I wanted, that was not one of them.

PLIMPTOV *exits.*

ORLO: He is a fool.

CATHERINE: A good looking one.

ORLO: Of course. I just—

CATHERINE: What?

ORLO: Imagining the inanity of his conversation.

CATHERINE: I doubt you could. I have you for conversation, and the bodies for when I want to get lost for a moment. So what are these pressing matters?

ORLO: Sewage.

CATHERINE: Of course. I have read Kayov's report, he is…

ORLO: A moron.

CATHERINE: You are being kind as usual.

ORLO: Letters from Voltaire and Diderot thanking you for your correspondence and support.

CATHERINE: Oh wonderful, it's like cold beer on a hot day, reading these two. Oh, I have written a piece on the future of taxation which I wish to be published. I just want to start the process.

ORLO: The process being, get them enraged?

CATHERINE: Enraged dies down, then they talk and chatter like fishwives, then there is acceptance.

ORLO: Not always.

CATHERINE: Often. Let us begin it, then. I must go to the girls' school later this week. A merchant's daughter starts there.

ORLO: I know. It is grumbled about at court.

CATHERINE: But celebrated in cottages all over Russia. For what is she, Orlo? For women, she is like the star of Bethlehem that girls all over Russia can see above them, shining and beckoning them to something more.

ORLO: I believe that is what they are grumbling about, yes.

CATHERINE: Will you come?

ORLO: Thursday is a long day with the generals.

CATHERINE: I have shifted it. It is now a long night with the generals. They will be drunk, but I will not miss the school, and I will not let them decide our course alone. There is so much Rooster and Cock about them. They have three vodkas and inevitably decide they will take France.

ORLO: Thankfully they generally pass out and forget that by morning.

CATHERINE: I would be happier if we just worked out a way to end the one we are stuck in. So we will go to the school together. It will be good for you to be surrounded by young women, Orlo. Your blood may flow out of your brain and in a different direction for a change.

ORLO: I may get dizzy.

CATHERINE: I shall hold your hand. You will be fine.

DIDI, Catherine's son, enters, dressed resplendently.

DIDI: Mother—

CATHERINE: Ah Didi, you have returned, how was the country?

DIDI: I am furious, you must give me something to do.

CATHERINE: Hand me that orange, will you?

Slightly baffled, he gives it her.

Good lad. Well done. That be all?

DIDI: Something serious, something—

CATHERINE: You are in a state?!

DIDI: Yes, I am in a state. I was out riding and stopped at an inn for a cooling beer, and… I was made wait…

Beat.

CATHERINE: Then?

DIDI: No then! That is it! As if I was an ordinary person, an Orlo, a dog. I was speechless.

CATHERINE: I wish I'd been there.

DIDI: Funny, Maman. He had no idea who I am! What is the point of being part of the royal family, if no-one knows who I am?!

ORLO: Maybe you should get a special hat.

DIDI: What?

ORLO: Like a prince's hat. So people would recognise you.

CATHERINE: A crown even.

ORLO: You have a crown. Wear it.

CATHERINE: Then you would get the respect I earned for you.

DIDI: Ah yes, sardonic parlour. Why did I feel I would be heard here? I would like to be known. I would like to be famous. You are, I am not.

CATHERINE: Didi, a man made you wait for a drink, assuming you were not you. Deal with it. Besides, we are trying to break down barriers between classes.

DIDI: Yes I know! I just don't know why! What is the point of being us, if we are to treated like them?

CATHERINE: We are all Russians.

DIDI: Yes, Mother, I have heard this speech, I had it with my tea my whole childhood.

CATHERINE: You could concern yourself with matters other than yourself.

DIDI: I would if you would die and let me!

ORLO: Sir!

CATHERINE: You are cross?

DIDI: Yes!

CATHERINE: It is a shame. You can go. We will inform you of my death immediately it transpires.

DIDI: Mother, I did not mean to—

CATHERINE: It is fine. I said go. We have work. Now.

DIDI *exits.*

ORLO: All my talks about equality and fraternity and liberty and the equality of man, and the nature of life and how one must truly live it for a purpose, somehow all that child heard was, 'I can have whatever I want'.

CATHERINE: Really? I feel like once it wasn't like that. Or am I getting old?

ORLO: Of course not.

CATHERINE: So the grey hair and wrinkles aren't really there.

ORLO: No more than my sagging gut and deaf ear.

CATHERINE: Then I will have that mirror broken for its impudence.

NATALIE, *Catherine's daughter in her early twenties, enters.*

NATALIE: Oh Mother, Orlo.

CATHERINE: Natalie, you are back, hopefully in better form than your brother.

NATALIE: Oh Mother, it is terrible.

CATHERINE: What is?

NATALIE: As we came into the city, seven carriages piled up, bodies and blood all over the road.

CATHERINE: Was anyone killed?

NATALIE: I do not know, they would not let us stop.

CATHERINE: Oh dear.

NATALIE: We must do something.

CATHERINE: Of course. I will send someone to find out what happened.

NATALIE: No. I mean we must outlaw it at once?

CATHERINE: Horses, accidents or carriages?

NATALIE: Carriages!

CATHERINE: How would we get around?

NATALIE: We would walk, as God intended.

CATHERINE: Oh, is that what God intended? So you are still in constant communication then? You and God?

ORLO: Catherine. She is shaken.

NATALIE: I am shaken by my mother's mocking tone, and General coldness in the face of a horrible story of death at her doorstep.

CATHERINE: I feel a sermon coming on. Maybe we should sit and order in some food.

NATALIE: It just draws attention to the fact you are lost.

CATHERINE: Other than being dizzy with your Godly bubble and squeak I know quite where I am. You are the most infernal girl.

NATALIE: And you are arrogance itself. You are God's servant. We must be as the lambs, meek before the sword.

CATHERINE: But not as the pedestrians before the carriages.

NATALIE: It is our duty to keep our subjects safe.

CATHERINE: I have freed people to live their lives, I cannot preoccupy myself with stopping their deaths. That is God's domain.

ORLO: Fate casts straws into the wind, occasionally one of them takes out an eye.

CATHERINE: So poetic, Orlo.

ORLO: I try.

NATALIE: I get a chill from you two.

CATHERINE: I have cured smallpox, freed the serfs, introduced democratic reforms, and kept corruption down to merely massive proportions. I cannot direct the traffic as well.

NATALIE: It is your cynicism that upsets me, Mother.

CATHERINE: Have a drink. Champagne?

NATALIE: It does not seem appropriate to wash down the bile of grief and horror with champagne.

CATHERINE: But surely you will not object to toasting the lives of those departed.

NATALIE: You are so clever, Mother.

CATHERINE: I am, it's true. So cheers and welcome back.

NATALIE: And to think I was so excited to come and tell you my... that I ran barefoot through the grass this morning, felt the tips of the grass licking my feet at the sheer elation at seeing you and speaking to you of...

CATHERINE: Of what, darling?

NATALIE: And now, you have ruined it!

She runs from the room.

ORLO: Why did I never have children?

CATHERINE: That girl.

ORLO: She reminds me of you. Incandescently beautiful, slightly mad.

CATHERINE: She has no wit. No... and her skin... it is so soft and pale it makes me want to punch her face.

MARIAL enters.

I did not call you.

MARIAL: Natalie is crying, that is the usual sign tea is over with.

She starts clearing up.

ORLO: What do you want to do about the Chechens?

CATHERINE: I will meet with their representatives.

ORLO: There is a report.

CATHERINE: I have read it. I... Marial, you are fussing. Which means you have something to say but do not know if you should say it.

MARIAL: I do not know whether I want to.

CATHERINE: Then I will have it beaten out of you.

MARIAL: You outlawed the beating of servants.

CATHERINE: Possibly a hasty move.

MARIAL: It was when you were young and blood still pumped in your heart.

CATHERINE: Droll. I was going to free you all. Remember that.

MARIAL: Indeed.

ORLO: Lost that one.

CATHERINE: One day I will.

MARIAL: I am hearing things.

CATHERINE: Are you hearing them as obtusely as you are saying them?

MARIAL: There are murmurings of a coup.

ORLO: There are always murmurings. I keep watchful vigilance. I hear nothing.

MARIAL: You are not listening in the right place.

CATHERINE: Where should he be listening?

MARIAL: The children.

CATHERINE: What? No.

MARIAL: It is just what I am hearing.

CATHERINE: It is ridiculous. My children would not.

MARIAL: I am sure you are right.

She exits with the tea tray as CATHERINE *watches.*

SCENE NINETEEN

Didi's chambers.

DIDI *stands next to a stuffed bear. The bear has a book shoved in its mouth.* DIDI *smiles a few different ways.* CATHERINE *enters.*

DIDI: Mother?

CATHERINE: Darling. What are you doing?

DIDI: I am having my portrait painted.

CATHERINE: Why is there a bear with a book in its mouth?

DIDI: It is a symbol.

CATHERINE: You hate bears that read and will not stand for them.

DIDI: No, I am both a hunter and a man of poetry.

CATHERINE: Of course. I apologise for before.

DIDI: You do? It is fine.

CATHERINE: And this morning, on your return, you were angry and asked for your mother's death?

DIDI: Mother. I do not wish for your death.

CATHERINE: You warm a mother's heart.

DIDI: Still there is an upside for me when it happens. I couldn't ignore that.

CATHERINE: You would not be my son if you did not see it.

DIDI: Thank you. You gave me a compliment!

CATHERINE: Of course.

DIDI: I cannot remember the last, when I was eight maybe. You walked past me, looked back and said, 'Nice pants'.

CATHERINE: I'm sure there were others. Are you happy with the way things are, Didi? The way I am running things? Perhaps you have advice for me. I would welcome that.

DIDI: Really?

CATHERINE: Really. What would you do?

DIDI: I would stop the war, of course.

CATHERINE: Why?

DIDI: People die. It is sad.

CATHERINE: True, but I cannot rule on what is sad and what is not sad. I agree there is a certain vivid pointlessness to the deaths in wars, but they are often necessary, despite it.

DIDI: I think you should stop it.

CATHERINE: Why? I would like to know why, your reasons, the basis for your position.

DIDI: You would?

CATHERINE: I would.

DIDI: All right. Well, when I was a kid, a General came to report to you from the front, he had a wound in his neck and I couldn't stop staring at it. When all of a sudden a maggot wiggled out of it.

Beat.

CATHERINE: A maggot?

DIDI: White one. It really put me off war.

CATHERINE: So it is not a moral or philosophical position, not even cowardice, it just makes you kind of squeamish. War.

DIDI: I saw a maggot crawl out of a man's neck! It was gross, it turned my stomach, that is why!

CATHERINE: And if the maggot had done a small dance perhaps that amused you, you may well be for war?

DIDI: So you came to make fun of me. I'm sorry, I thought you actually wanted to talk to me.

CATHERINE: I do. I do. Anything else? Besides the war, anything else you would change?

DIDI: No, pretty much as is, is good for me. I am mostly happy, and once my portrait is out there, coupled with rumours of my derring-do in the war. Which I have men spreading.

CATHERINE: Your derring-do in the war you are against and will not go near?

DIDI: Yes, well, people like a good story, me winning battles is a good one.

CATHERINE: It is a brilliant idea.

DIDI: Thank you, Mother.

Beat.

CATHERINE: I was given a bear once. A man brought it to my quarters.

Beat.

DIDI: Not your best anecdote, Mother.

CATHERINE: Of course, darling. And Peter. I like your pants.

She exits. A GENERAL *enters.*

DIDI: How did I do?

GENERAL: You were a model of confusion and dissonance, sir.

DIDI: Excellent. I do love my mother. But she does not love me. I hope I am not doing this because I am angry at her.

GENERAL: Sir, you act for the good of all Russians. It is a selfless act.

DIDI: She has a heart like flint, she will not be hurt.

GENERAL: Of course not. We hope to inter her in the summer palace. Hopefully without bloodshed.

DIDI: Excellent. I should have a musket.

GENERAL: What?

DIDI: For the portrait. The people are stupid. What if they do not understand the portrait and think the bear died of natural causes?

SCENE TWENTY

Natalie's chambers.

CATHERINE *enters.* NATALIE *continues praying.* CATHERINE *finally picks up a tea cup and drops it, shattering it.*

CATHERINE: Oh, I'm sorry. Just me, Empress of Russia. Sorry to interrupt.

NATALIE: Mother. I am sorry I was angry at you this morning. While I was praying, I searched my heart.

CATHERINE: Find anything?

NATALIE: Compassion for you.

CATHERINE: Keep it for those who die in carriage accidents or religious wars, darling. I do not need it, nor deserve it.

NATALIE: I do not want to fight with you.

CATHERINE: Nor I you.

NATALIE: Let's hug.

CATHERINE: Hug? Why?

NATALIE: It is an expression of love. And it is silent. It will suit us better.

CATHERINE: Well said.

They hug.

I did not take you seriously this morning.

NATALIE: Why not?

CATHERINE: Honestly?

NATALIE: Of course.

CATHERINE: What you were saying was stupid.

NATALIE: Oh, for the love of—

CATHERINE: You asked.

NATALIE: We are so different Mother, and I do worry so for you.

CATHERINE: For me, in what way?

NATALIE: Your soul.

CATHERINE: Not a problem till I'm dead.

NATALIE: That could happen any day.

CATHERINE: Really? You have had a vision?

NATALIE: God could take any of us at any time.

CATHERINE: But me specifically? Posit a guess?

NATALIE: The sexual deviantness, your behaviour infects the whole court.

CATHERINE: I have a clean bill of health, doctor will swear.

NATALIE: That is not what I meant, morally, spiritually.

CATHERINE: Oh, of course.

NATALIE: They say you had congress with a horse.

CATHERINE: It is not true! The horse wanted to, but I refused, and neigh means neigh.

NATALIE: You cannot take me seriously.

CATHERINE: You are too earnest. Don't you want to have some fun? You are young and free and can be and do anything.

NATALIE: I do. I am.

CATHERINE: This is it, what you want to do? Be a frigid pain in the arse?

NATALIE: Yes. I mean… I want to be me! Which is… Oh, for God's sake. I could shake you.

CATHERINE: I would not, who knows what will fall out? If you believe the rumours, I have a wood mouse living in my vagina.

NATALIE: You are the Queen! God's representative on earth. It will not do.

CATHERINE: What will do?

NATALIE: Something else. Something better.

CATHERINE: You would not let people in your ear who would bring me down, Nat?

NATALIE: No. Of course not.

CATHERINE: You would never lie to me I hope. Between us is much strife and bickering and differences but we are always honest and that is a cherished thing.

NATALIE: Yes. It is.

CATHERINE: I have your word?

> NATALIE *nods.* CATHERINE *goes to leave.*

NATALIE: And if I did, or was, it would not be me, it would be on God's behalf, it would be an intercession and not diminish my love for you in any way. But it would be in God's service. If I was given a sign to act. A sign that could not be ignored.

CATHERINE: I see.

NATALIE: Mother, do you not wish for love, pure and beautiful in all its forms? For your life to be nothing but an endless expression of love and nought else?

CATHERINE: Of course.

NATALIE: I have found it and pure it is, and glorious, on a patch of grass, leaves falling on me. I and this extraordinary man became as one. And it was transcendent. I am not a prude. I know how it should be, I have had it, and what you have saddens and sickens me. And not for God but out of my love for you. For he gave me a sign of something else. To pursue it, to spread it, and I must be true to that.

> *Beat.*

CATHERINE: *You had sex?!*

NATALIE: Yes I did. I am in love, Mother. In love.

CATHERINE: You are?

NATALIE: That is what I wished to tell you, but then what with the carriage accident and you and Orlo being appalling.

CATHERINE: Who is he?

> VAL *(played by the same actor who played Hermes) walks in. He looks exactly like Hermes. Even his dress is similar.*

VAL: I guess that's my cue.

NATALIE: Val, my darling. This is my mother.

VAL: Empress. It is an honour. Valerie Girgoriev, my family own estates around Kiev.

They wait for CATHERINE *to respond. But she just stares at him.*

Since I was a young man I heard tales of your greatness, and what you have done for Russia... Also Natalie speaks... of you often... I brought you a peach, Nat. We could share it, though... if you like, Empress... I do... Nat?

NATALIE: Mother, you are being rude.

CATHERINE: I am sorry. I... suddenly feel unwell.

NATALIE: What is it?

VAL: Can I get you anything?

NATALIE: Mother, you are staring.

CATHERINE: I must go.

    She exits in a flurry.

SCENE TWENTY-ONE

Catherine's quarters.

CATHERINE *sits on the floor, cards for solitaire in front of her, which she plays relentlessly.* MARIAL *comes in with tea.* CATHERINE *wipes at her eyes.*

MARIAL: You saw him, then?

CATHERINE: You knew? You did not think to tell?

MARIAL: Would it have helped?

CATHERINE: No.

MARIAL: You have been crying.

CATHERINE: Sobbing, more accurately.

MARIAL: Oh, dear Catherine.

CATHERINE: I am lost.

MARIAL: It is not him.

CATHERINE: Of course it is him.

MARIAL: It is... a coincidence.

CATHERINE: A coincidence?! Marial, you do not believe that. You are a village witch, always reading tea leaves or signs in the swirl of chicken livers on a plate.

MARIAL: And you have always lectured me on the ridiculousness of these things. Perhaps it has finally seeped in.

CATHERINE: It is him. Back to punish me.

MARIAL: We—

CATHERINE: Do not lie to me. I need you now.

Beat.

MARIAL: He has come. We do not know the why of it.

CATHERINE: These damn tears. I cannot stop leaking! It is absurd. Twenty-four years ago.

MARIAL: It is not the when it was, but the what it was.

CATHERINE: He used to come to me in my dreams. His shirt drenched in blood, tears on his cheeks, stand there and stare at me, not reproachfully, just baffled, uncomprehending.

MARIAL: You have done great things.

CATHERINE: Maybe not worth what I did, not to me and not to him. Maybe that is why he is back.

MARIAL: To punish you? He loved you, why would he want that?

CATHERINE: Because I am a murderous slut and I deserve it.

MARIAL: He loved you.

CATHERINE: Which makes what I did the worse. Makes what I did unforgivable.

ORLO *enters. He sees them sitting on the floor together.*

ORLO: What is it?

CATHERINE: The end, Orlo. I think it might be the end.

SCENE TWENTY-TWO

The ballroom.

NATALIE *and* VAL *are dancing.*

VAL: And we touch, and we turn, and we touch, and we kiss.

He grabs her and kisses her.

NATALIE: I doubt that is part of the dance.

VAL: Well, my mother taught me it and she said it was.

NATALIE: Val! That is not true.

VAL: No it is not. I am just addicted to seeing you shocked, it is almost when you are at your most beautiful.

NATALIE: You are a beast.

VAL: And you a princess.

NATALIE: That is fact, rather than compliment. Try harder.

ORLO *and* CATHERINE *appear. They watch and listen to them.*

VAL: I shall not try at all. We do not need to. It is fate.

NATALIE: Oh my God! I feel exactly the same way, you say things and it's like they are things that were in my head, I almost wasn't aware of!

VAL: It is either love, or I am sent by Satan.

NATALIE: Don't say that. It is a bad joke.

VAL: You know I do not believe in Satan.

NATALIE: You should, it grounds one.

VAL: Since I met you all I do is float.

NATALIE: There you go again! That is exactly what I was thinking. I have to remind myself of Satan to keep me grounded and fearful.

VAL: Fearful of what?

NATALIE: Right now, I can't for the life of me remember.

He laughs. He starts dancing with her again. ORLO *and* CATHERINE *are to one side where they are watching, unseen.*

ORLO: He is… him.

CATHERINE: He said he would haunt me. My God, Orlo.

ORLO: It is just a…

CATHERINE: A what? I would like to know?

ORLO: I… Are you all right?

CATHERINE: My daughter wants to kill me, a ghost has come to call on me!

ORLO: It is a troubling time, I grant that. I do not believe this about Nat.

CATHERINE: She is a zealot.

ORLO: It is not the Nat I know.

CATHERINE: I am evil and must be removed.

ORLO: Then he has been in her ear.

CATHERINE: That's the least of it.

ORLO: You are wrong about her, this is Nat, she is a butterfly, an angel.

CATHERINE: She is not twelve anymore, Uncle Orlo, wake up.

ORLO: She is an innocent. It is her heart. It does not change.

> *In the middle of the room...*

NATALIE: Can I suck your thing again?

VAL: Of course.

ORLO: Maybe she has grown up.

> NATALIE *drops to her knees.* CATHERINE *enters.*

CATHERINE: My darling daughter, do you never tire of praying?

NATALIE: Mother.

VAL: Empress.

CATHERINE: Dear Val, I was struck dumb last time we met. I did not know my daughter was in love. It surprised me.

VAL: No apology is necessary.

NATALIE: This is Orlo.

VAL: Ah, Orlo, it is an honour, she does love you dearly, I have heard a lot of you.

ORLO: I am touched. It is a pleasure to meet you.

CATHERINE: Natalie, Orlo needs your help with...

> ORLO *is lost for words.*

We cannot think of a reason. The hell with it, I am Empress, I would like to mercilessly quiz your beau here.

NATALIE: Mother. No.

VAL: It is fine.

NATALIE: It is not, she will peel you like an onion.

CATHERINE: It will be more an analogy involving looking through entrails. But she has it right.

VAL: As anyone who loved their daughter would do. Let us gut me like a fish and see what spills forth.

NATALIE: It is no joke, Val, she has a talent for turning bizarre analogies into fact. She is a murderous slut.

ORLO: Natalie! You are wrong to say that.

NATALIE: Because it is not true?

CATHERINE: She has you, Orlo, back off lest she pull your wings off.

NATALIE: Why do you do this to me?

CATHERINE: I have no idea what you are talking about.

NATALIE: That has been the case since I was seven.

CATHERINE: I would have said five, but then we rarely agree.

VAL: It is good to join a spirited family.

ORLO: Do not get ahead of yourself, sir. You are a long way from the altar.

VAL: And you are related in what capacity, sir?

CATHERINE: We are related by blood, but not the sort you are thinking of.

ORLO: More the sort we have spilt together. But have a lovely chat, I will send Marial with madelines and tea.

NATALIE: Orlo, you are as bad as her sometimes.

CATHERINE: It is true, Orlo, you really are.

> NATALIE *kisses* VAL *hard on the lips.*

NATALIE: Orlo! Come. We will walk in the garden.

> NATALIE *exits.* ORLO *follows.* VAL *stands.* CATHERINE *looks at him. She doesn't speak, but becomes kind of transfixed.*

VAL: You cannot stop staring at me.

CATHERINE: Do not flatter yourself.

VAL: I do not find it flattering, more disconcerting. I fear you want to eat me.

CATHERINE: I do not. [*Beat.*] I… would like to touch your face.

VAL: Touch my face?

CATHERINE: Would that be okay?

VAL: I suppose so.

> *She comes to him, puts her hand on his face and closes her eyes.*

I—

CATHERINE: Please don't speak.

> *Beat. She opens her eyes and looks at him. She kisses him softly but firmly on the lips, then steps away, a bit at sea within herself.*

VAL: Not quite as tough a grilling as I expected.

CATHERINE: Why are you here?

VAL: It is the centre of things, and your daughter is here.

CATHERINE: Yes of course. What do you want with my daughter?

VAL: Marriage, children, sex, fame, money, political power, the order's more random than sequential of importance.

CATHERINE: Not quite the difficult nut to crack, are you?

VAL: Why waste our time, I doubt you're easily lied to. Even though, I am a good liar, but eighty percent of successful lying is actually dependant on the other person's delusions and secret desires. You can only really lie to someone who is already lying to themselves. It is like a pile of hats. They already have a pile of hats, so they barely notice you have thrown another one on the pile, since if you asked them directly they would deny even owning a hat.

CATHERINE: Dazzling.

VAL: I know. Sometimes I find my brilliance alarming.

CATHERINE: And what of your troubling self doubt?

VAL: I seem to have it in check for the moment.

CATHERINE: Indeed. So do you love my daughter?

VAL: I did not take you for a romantic.

CATHERINE: Do not mistake the fact I neither like nor understand my daughter. I will happily leave here with your tongue in a jar to protect her.

VAL: I doubt she would approve the removal of my tongue. She is quite attached to it.

CATHERINE: You are relentlessly confident.

VAL: Is it annoying?

CATHERINE: A little. And helps you evade my question.

VAL: She loves me, nothing you say can change that.

CATHERINE: What do you want?

VAL: To be Emperor.

CATHERINE: You aim to save Russia?

VAL: You already did that. I aim to keep it going.

CATHERINE: Don't try to flatter me. You should know your place.

VAL: You have taught us we do not need to. We can be and have what we want.

CATHERINE: Forty years of speaking of Voltaire and Rousseau and all you children heard was you can get what you want.

VAL: I suppose so. As legend has it, you did.

CATHERINE: I did it for Russia!

VAL: And Russia thanks you.

CATHERINE: But now you want me dead?

VAL: No. But I cannot wait forever. I am twenty-three.

She laughs.

CATHERINE: I could have you killed right now. Yell the order. And in sixty seconds you would be pulling your last breath into your cut throat.

VAL: She would hate you forever.

CATHERINE: She already does.

VAL: You won't do anything.

CATHERINE: You are sure?

VAL: I can tell by the way you look at me. I do not know why. But you cannot lay a hand to me.

He slaps her softly across the face. She stares at him, then waits. She stares weakly at him.

As I thought. Good day, Your Highness.

VAL *exits.*

CATHERINE: I will cut your eyes out and have them set into rings!

She does not move.

SCENE TWENTY-THREE

ORLO *waits with* MARIAL. *He is struggling with a bottle in an agitated way.* MARIAL *takes it from him and pops the cork.* ORLO *looks at her.* CATHERINE *enters.*

CATHERINE: He wants me dead. He does not love Nat. He's sure he will win.

ORLO: He is wrong! We will swat him like a fucking fly!

CATHERINE: He has come and I cannot fight it.

ORLO: I will fight it, then! If he is what you say he is then he must be dealt with. Why will you not?

MARIAL: It is as plain as the nose on his face and the limpid eyes in his head.

CATHERINE: Old woman.

ORLO: It is not him!

CATHERINE: For Nat. I will not break her heart. She loves him.

ORLO: Two months ago she loved her rabbit and would die for it. Last Tuesday she ate it in a pie! She will move on. People move on!

CATHERINE: You would not understand.

ORLO: Because I have no heart. For old Orlo is a bloodless freak who does not want or desire. Or love.

CATHERINE: Pretty much. She will see it. In time.

ORLO: In time? You do not let a viper into your bed. Or maybe you do, as you pretty much let anything into bed.

CATHERINE: I am to be punished! It is... fate.

ORLO: Oh my God... you are talking like some village idiot. Shall we write to Voltaire and ask his opinion of this coincidence being read as fate.

MARIAL: It is a terrible thing to lose love young, they die perfect. When they die old, you remember them fondly, their laughter, kindness, touch, but it is tempered by their rank smell, interest in figurines, and the way they kissed you after a big night on beer and herring. The way my man used to fart, Jesus Christ, I swear he killed our firstborn.

CATHERINE: Yes, Marial. Thank you for your input.

MARIAL: He loved you. Why would he want to punish you?

CATHERINE: Because I am a murderous slut.

MARIAL: You have been punished. I have seen it every day.

CATHERINE: I have grieved, it is different.

ORLO: What about Plimptov? That is not punishment?

CATHERINE: What?

ORLO: Or any of the others. You choose this, I have seen it before me for thirty years.

MARIAL: As have I.

CATHERINE: You are going to gang up on me?

MARIAL: It will take two of us and a shovel to reshape your mind.

ORLO: But let us give it a try. Plimptov, Aransky…

MARIAL: The children's fathers.

CATHERINE: Natalie's father was darling… he was Retovsky right?

MARIAL: You have turned your back on love.

CATHERINE: That is not true.

ORLO: You have let these animals have you.

CATHERINE: I like to get off, for God's sake. Who does not? Liars, that is who. As for the other. I did not find love again, maybe that is all.

> DIDI *rides in on a tricycle. He hands his mother a copy of his picture.*

DIDI: First copy for you, Maman.

CATHERINE: Didi, I cannot be cheered by your idiocy now.

DIDI: Of course. I will leave. You know, Mother, I have spent my life being sent from rooms by you. If I was a more sensitive man…

CATHERINE: Didi. I am…

DIDI: Mother, please. You are you.

CATHERINE: I am not sure what that means. But it does not sound like a compliment.

DIDI: You are you. I struggle with your youness. But am resolved to it as well. One does not expect a piano to be a cow, now does one? One may want it to, one may hit it with a broom, but it will tinkle and it will never give milk. You see.

CATHERINE: What does that mean?

DIDI: There has been a pane of ice between us my whole life, eventual one tires of a frostbitten face.

CATHERINE: I see.

DIDI: I have wept and seen you in the doorway of the room staring at me. And I have waited for you to cross that twelve steps of floor to me, to hold me.

CATHERINE: I never did?

DIDI: No. But you tinkle, you do not give milk. Tinkle? You are a symphony, Mother, you are great and you will be remembered in history.

CATHERINE: Didi, you are a—

DIDI: I am a disappointment. I know that. Let's not embarrass ourselves by pretending it is not so. I am more jew's harp than harpsichord.

> DIDI *exits.*

CATHERINE: I do not understand why they feel I do not love them! That I do not want the best for them! [*Beat.*] I also do not understand the awkward silence that better have its pregnancy aborted with haste.

MARIAL: They do not feel it, because they do not see it.

CATHERINE: Orlo?

ORLO: You have always been strangely brusque with them.

MARIAL: Short.

ORLO: Cavalier.

MARIAL: Cruel.

CATHERINE: I see.

ORLO: I'm sorry.

CATHERINE: Do not apologise. [*Beat.*] I did not… deserve them.

ORLO: What do you mean?

CATHERINE: I had them so I would love something again. It could not be another man, that would be like saying he did not exist. He did not matter. That I had not done anything. But if I had the children it would free that part of me. But it didn't. I could not give myself it. When they came to me I rejected them, when I wanted to go to them I clamped myself shut. And then it became something I didn't do, it was something I was until I forgot it had happened. I have hurt them so much, and doubled the punishment I envisaged. And maybe that's right, for me. But it is not right for them.

ORLO: Catherine, you have nothing to atone for.

CATHERINE: We both know that is not true.

ORLO: We have transformed Russia!

CATHERINE: We have failed as often as we succeeded. When we started I thought we could just sit everyone down round the fire and read to them from Voltaire and Montesquieu and they would just suddenly go, 'Oh, I see', and get up and embrace as members of a common family. But it is not and was not so, we drag them inch by inch like a rain-soaked ox up a muddy hill.

ORLO: That is the job and we are good at it.

CATHERINE: They do not want it most of the time.

ORLO: And she and he would kick the ox back down the hill and suddenly we would be knee-deep in the mud of superstition and fear.

CATHERINE: People do not care! Do you not see that? Their lives aren't precious to them, they do not know how to use them, all the freedoms I wrenched into being for them they use to further their greed and avarice. I took a life that was precious, from a man who loved it and knew how to live, for them.

ORLO: You have done so much good, saved so many against one man.

CATHERINE: It is not a ledger, Orlo, it will never add up.

SCENE TWENTY-FOUR

Natalie's chambers.

NATALIE *sits writing.* CATHERINE *enters.*

CATHERINE: He is lovely.

NATALIE: What?

CATHERINE: Val. I am very happy for you.

NATALIE: You are?

CATHERINE: You must marry at once.

NATALIE: I…

CATHERINE: Seem surprised.

NATALIE: Yes, I thought you—

CATHERINE: Would hate him. You have always had a fixed idea of your mother. It is an impediment to our relationship.

NATALIE: He liked you very much as well.

CATHERINE: You seem disconcerted by that?

NATALIE: No. I am pleased.

CATHERINE: I realise you both aim to unseat me, but what if I were to abdicate for you and him?

NATALIE: You would do that?

CATHERINE: Perhaps if I could train you both. If—

NATALIE: We do not need to be led.

CATHERINE: It is true, he has strong ideas.

NATALIE: As do I.

CATHERINE: What about Didi, though? He will be annoyed. Remember when he used to kill all his pets?

NATALIE: It was a phase.

CATHERINE: Which only stopped when we stopped giving him pets. I worry about him. Ah well, you may have to kill him.

NATALIE: Then we will.

CATHERINE: Good. You will need to. But that is what it takes. I can see why you are inspired by Val. He kissed me and it was really…

NATALIE: What?

CATHERINE: A chaste kiss on the lips. Well, a little tongue I suppose. Stirred the old downstairs.

NATALIE: You are disgusting. He is not one of your rutting herd and do not try and make it so. He is an exalted soul.

CATHERINE: Yes. Well, you have my blessing, that is all I am saying.

NATALIE: I don't think it is all you are saying, but I cannot work out what it is you are saying.

CATHERINE: Old habits die hard, darling. I am trying to give in. To you.

NATALIE: Why?

CATHERINE: I see signs around me that tell me it may be so. You seem intent on your course. And I do not know how to fight it. But maybe I can be quick enough to get out of the way before I am run over.

NATALIE: I am glad.

CATHERINE: I am glad you are glad. If you were disappointed I would've really been hurt.

NATALIE: I did not want to kill you.

CATHERINE: Nor I you.

They look at each other a beat. NATALIE *rushes to hug her.*

NATALIE: Thank you, Mother. It will be wonderful, I promise.

CATHERINE: If you let me help you with it, it is complex and—

NATALIE: It will be good for you to see Russia return to God's laws.

CATHERINE: I suppose so.

NATALIE: I aim to be so many things you weren't.

CATHERINE: Nobody's perfect, surely not me.

NATALIE: You will see, I aim to uplift us to a righteous caring.

CATHERINE: God's law?

NATALIE: I have a purpose. You have told me all my life to have one.

CATHERINE: Well, I meant…

NATALIE: One you approved of?

CATHERINE: Pretty much. Yes.

NATALIE: There is so much to do. I must share this with Val.

CATHERINE: You stupid! Stupid, stupid girl!

NATALIE: What?

CATHERINE: He is a liar and a fraud and he does not love you and he has come to cause me pain and to punish me!

NATALIE *laughs at her.*

NATALIE: You are the most hilarious, most obvious creature in the history of obvious hilarious creatures which is long and includes unicorns and ligers.

CATHERINE: Oh, for God's sake. You have to believe me.

NATALIE *laughs.*

NATALIE: I knew you would try something.

CATHERINE: Stop it! I have no reason to lie, what possible reason would I have, Nat?

NATALIE: The most obvious. I am happy.

CATHERINE: You are deluded. It is not the same. Darling, I know it is hard to accept.

NATALIE *laughs again.*

NATALIE: Stop it! Stop it! My sides. It's hurting them.

CATHERINE: Nat!

NATALIE: You just cannot stand that I could have something beautiful. I saw the way you looked at him. You have these rutting pigs come in and service you, maul you, and you could not bear that I have something exalted and pure.

CATHERINE: I… the way I looked at him is… why would you think that I do not want you to be happy? Look, he is your first, it is important.

NATALIE: He is my first and only, he is my destiny.

CATHERINE: And my fate. He is certainly multipurpose.

NATALIE: What?

CATHERINE: It is nothing. I do not believe in destiny or fate. We are the authors of our own script.

NATALIE: That would leave God somewhat redundant, Mother.

CATHERINE: You said it. Let us leave that hot coal, for once we shall not toss it between us.

NATALIE: No, let us toss it. He is a sign to me from God. I have waited all my life to find someone who filled this empty hole in me.

CATHERINE: Call it a vagina, darling. Euphemisms are for four-year-olds.

NATALIE: You have to degrade everything.

CATHERINE: Why not please your mother instead of God?

NATALIE: I have discovered it is easier to please God. I understand fate is at work, he has come and he is a sign to me to rise and fulfill my destiny.

CATHERINE: He is your sign! Him! He is not fit to be in that body, to wear that face. He is not a sign! He is your first fuck! That is all. He fucked you under a tree. He opened doors to a part of you, you had denied your whole life. And you cannot just say, 'I like to be fucked hard and dirty', because that would make you like me. It has to be a sign from God. It is not. It is sex. Wonderful old fucking. God's gift to keep us going to work each day.

NATALIE: You are wrong. It is a great love, extraordinary and transcendent. You would not understand it.

CATHERINE *slaps her.*

CATHERINE: Do not tell me about great love, I know about great love! You do not! I have loved every day of my life like a burning in my chest.

NATALIE: Who?! Who have you loved? Who? Not those animals you let ravage you, the boys you deflower, them?

CATHERINE: I have kept my heart…

NATALIE: For who? From us, but for who?

> *Beat.*

CATHERINE: A man. A man I loved who I let them kill.

NATALIE: What?

CATHERINE: I chose a great life over a great love. And have punished myself for it ever since. I did this thing and the idea I was a person who could do that was abhorrent to me, I could not embrace it. I would not. I wanted love and when I had you and Didi I thought maybe I could… I wanted to love you, but I could not give myself that. I have made you suffer for that and it has bent my life into this misshapen form where my daughter loathes me. You are right. I have failed you. I would like to start again.

NATALIE: It is too late. Despite your touching story of how you killed the man you loved.

CATHERINE: It is not. We are here at the spot, we can change everything. I would like to love you, teach you, I would like us to be great. Maybe it would be as easy as reaching our hands toward the other.

NATALIE: So I take your hand the once you offer it, despite the thousand times you have spurned mine.

CATHERINE: It would be damn Christian of you, I agree.

NATALIE: Maybe I am not such a good Christian after all.

CATHERINE: He does not love you, Nat.

NATALIE: Just because you cannot does mean no-one else can.

CATHERINE: That's not true.

NATALIE: But I have believed that was the case. Until him.

CATHERINE: I do love you.

NATALIE: Then I will be wary of my life if your history is anything to go by.

CATHERINE: What can I do?

NATALIE: You came to give in to me, remember?

CATHERINE: You are not ready. And he is the smallpox returned.

NATALIE: Then we must fight, mustn't we?

CATHERINE: He is—

NATALIE: You cannot dupe me, Mother, my gaze is frosty, and I finally, reluctantly, yet somewhat inevitably, see your heart for what it is. And I have thrown my love against that wall for too long. I now have Val, and I will have Russia as well.

CATHERINE: I will show you who Val really is.

NATALIE: Do your worst. For I would like to watch your face fall as it encounters real goodness.

SCENE TWENTY-FIVE

Catherine's quarters.

MARIAL *straightens some cushions several times.* CATHERINE *comes in.*

CATHERINE: Surely by now you know how they go?

MARIAL: It is my curse. Some people have syphilis, I have cushions. How will you do this?

CATHERINE: I will seduce him.

MARIAL: You cannot. She will hate you forever.

CATHERINE: I am aware of the cost.

MARIAL: Then why pay it? You are an extraordinary women, you could manufacture something she does not suspect, say a bad carriage accident, or just a brawl in a pub where he is run through.

CATHERINE: You may have been wasted as a maid.

MARIAL: No doubt. Why must you hurt her like this?

CATHERINE: He does not love her and one day she will see it and it will be too late, she will just think it is her fault it has disappeared and she will go mad chasing something that was never there and half her life will be ruined. She should know love! What it is like to be truly loved. I must give her the chance at that. No matter what.

MARIAL: You do not need to do this. You can spare yourself and her this. Why not take the easy way for once?

CATHERINE: The truth of the thing will not destroy her, believing the lie will.

MARIAL: I'm just saying, well-orchestrated carriage accident, everyone is spared the cost of the thing.

CATHERINE: No-one is ever spared the cost of a thing, Marial. Even if one tries to evade it, it comes and finds one and rips it from you in ways you cannot foresee or imagine.

MARIAL: She will not thank you for getting rid of him. She will fester like a suppurating wound.

CATHERINE: Yes, Marial. Thank you for the colour.

   MARIAL *exits.* VAL *enters.*

So we meet again?

VAL: Not such a random occurrence since you did send your guards to bring me here.

CATHERINE: You are a clever boy.

VAL: I am a man.

CATHERINE: Don't be so forceful. I will swoon, and possibly disrobe.

VAL: I'm sorry, I find myself wary around you.

CATHERINE: You said yourself there is nothing I can do to you. You saw that.

VAL: Is it true?

CATHERINE: Perhaps. Although there are many carriage accidents these days. Have you ever been to Venice, Val?

VAL: No.

CATHERINE: It is a freewheeling cads' paradise, the food is to live for, the women to die for and the air and light and buildings and water shimmer like you are in an hallucination had by Michelangelo. I need an ambassador there.

VAL: Do you?

CATHERINE: I don't imagine it would be a good town for a man with a wife, though. It may cramp his style. One should taste life unfettered, don't you think.

VAL: Who do I remind you of?

CATHERINE: That is not the business of—

VAL: I'm tying it in, humour me.

CATHERINE: A man.

VAL: A man you loved?

CATHERINE: Yes.

VAL: Who was he?

CATHERINE: It is not important.

VAL: What happened to him?

CATHERINE: He died.

VAL: How?

CATHERINE: It is not important! He died. I miss him. Our business is Venice. Is you leaving.

VAL: The way you look at me, wistful and lustful at once, it is quite something to be the subject of.

CATHERINE: Let us get back to Venice. Bolito misto and salsa verde are not to be missed.

VAL: I look like him?

CATHERINE: You are the image of him. It is… I can't look at you without…

VAL: Wanting me?

CATHERINE: Do not play with me.

VAL: Did you kill him?

CATHERINE: No … he was killed. Yes.

He goes to her and puts his hand on her face.

VAL: You think it is a coincidence I have come back.

CATHERINE: It is not you.

VAL: That I would leave you and never return, when I loved you as I did.

CATHERINE: Do not… Hermes, is it you?

VAL: It is.

CATHERINE: Why are…?

VAL: I have not come to punish you, but to taste you again.

CATHERINE: Oh God.

VAL: For I have missed you.

He pulls her to him.

CATHERINE: And I you. I sometimes taste apricot in the back of my throat.

VAL: Um… Okay.

CATHERINE *pushes him away suddenly.*

CATHERINE: You swine.

VAL: I would like to go to Venice. But maybe I would like to take a souvenir with me.

CATHERINE: You are my daughter's… it is obscene.

VAL: What if I did not speak? If I just said I was glad to be back with you. That I forgave you. That I wanted to touch you one last time, to feel us together for just a moment.

CATHERINE: No. I… she would… Natalie…

VAL: She already hates you. It would not be much more or less.

He touches her neck. He kisses her neck. CATHERINE *pushes* VAL *away. He laughs.* ORLO *enters, smacks him across the head with an iron candlestick, grabs him and throws him to the ground. He starts savagely choking him.*

ORLO: He will not touch you.

CATHERINE: Orlo, stop it! Stop it!

ORLO: No! You think I'd let him fuck you. Again.

CATHERINE: Orlo! It is not him!

He stops. VAL *writhes a little.*

ORLO: It is him. It is always him. In your heart. And me, what am I?

CATHERINE: Orlo.

ORLO: Yes, bloodless Orlo.

NATALIE *slowly walks out toward the body.*

NATALIE: You filthy slagheap of evil. You putrescent creeping demon. You and your charred black soul and your walnut heart. I hate you. I will hate you forever, I will fill my heart with hate until I drown us both in it.

CATHERINE: Oh, my baby, please do not.

NATALIE: Please do not? You ask something of me? You?

CATHERINE: That you do not let this ruin you. You know about Venice—

NATALIE: You tricked him!

CATHERINE: And you feel like a fool—

NATALIE: He loved me! He did!

CATHERINE: And you hate yourself for it.

NATALIE: You odious troll!

CATHERINE: I am sorry.

NATALIE: I want to kill you. My heart is filled with black blood and all I want is to kill you.

CATHERINE: Yes.

NATALIE: But…

> *She breaks down.* CATHERINE *goes to her and holds her.* NATALIE *struggles for a second and then gives in and holds her mother.*

No!

> *She runs from the room. Beat.* CATHERINE *sits on the floor.*

CATHERINE: [*looking at* ORLO] Twenty years you act without passion and you choose today.

ORLO: I am sorry.

> *Beat.*

CATHERINE: All this time?

ORLO: Yes. I felt I just did not… act. I told myself the things you tell yourself. That you were with those men, but I was closest to you.

CATHERINE: You were.

ORLO: I have asked nothing and given all.

CATHERINE: That is not love, Orlo.

ORLO: What about those late nights we worked five, six years after he died? We burned mountains of oil and drank litres of vodka getting ready the democratic reform conference. Late at night, in that room, talking feverishly and dreaming and planning and alive. You were alive, you had shaken free of the past for hours at a time, you were flying, you were you, utterly, extraordinarily you. Sometimes our hands would touch and a spark would flare between us and I would stand ready and looking into your eyes and I would watch as you turned from it and let it fall to the ground and burn up. Did I imagine that?

CATHERINE: Oh, Orlo. I was probably thinking of him.

ORLO: Oh.

CATHERINE: You are my dearest friend.

ORLO: [*nodding*] Of course. We need to have this body cleared away. I will attend to it, Empress.

He gets up and goes to exit.

CATHERINE: I could not let him go, because then…

ORLO: Yes?

CATHERINE: He would be gone.

SCENE TWENTY-SIX

A salon.

MARIAL *sets out the tea things.* NATALIE *comes in, a handsome young* COUNT, *who looks a lot like the young Orlo, by her side.*

COUNT: I enjoyed our walk.

NATALIE: And I the fuck we had when we stopped.

COUNT: Of course that was the highlight. I will be close by.

NATALIE: You had better be.

COUNT: I love it when you threaten me.

NATALIE: It does get the blood racing, doesn't it?

He departs. She goes and takes tea and sits, as CATHERINE *enters.*

CATHERINE: How was your walk?

NATALIE: Nature is a beautiful thing.

CATHERINE: Indeed it is. You will join me at the school today?

NATALIE: Is that a question or an order?

CATHERINE: A question.

NATALIE: Then I will. I would like to see their faces as the merchants' daughters finish term.

CATHERINE: We should not gloat. At least not openly.

NATALIE: I understand.

    ORLO enters.

ORLO: Natalie. Catherine.

NATALIE: Orlo. A madeleine.

ORLO: Thank you. We will leave shortly for the school. People are excited. Some by the idea of it. Some by the idea of throwing rocks at us because of it.

CATHERINE: How else would we know we've done good if someone did not want to hurl a rock?

ORLO: I will catch one and add it to the collection.

CATHERINE: Brilliant idea.

    DIDI arrives with a GENERAL.

DIDI: Mother, it is time.

CATHERINE: For what, Didi?

DIDI: For you to leave with my men, they will escort you to the summer house in Odessa. You will remain there. I will be Emperor.

CATHERINE: Why do you want this, Didi?

DIDI: I do not have to justify it to you, Mother.

CATHERINE: When I first came here a prince held a serf down in the courtyard and burnt his face with a hot blacksmith's iron. The man died. He had seven children. The prince was legally entitled to do that. He took tea with Peter that afternoon, a respected member of our court. Everyone acted as if nothing had happened. It was jovial, the atmosphere. But in our hearts, children. I saw something like soot falling into our souls and spreading a black stain. This was a country that had no love and no heart. I believed that we could find them in ourselves. I believe in people, I trust in people. I have battled my whole life to get them to trust themselves and each other. And have succeeded some and failed as well. Because as people we are so desperate to hand that responsibility onto another and there are plenty who will take it and abuse it. I took this because I had a thirst, a responsibility to something within that was bursting my veins, that to turn my back on would have left me with a bitter sense of betrayal. Didi, you want this because you are afraid. Afraid you are nothing. You cling to the way it is because you have no faith that you would have any of this if you were not born to it. And you are right. You would not. But do not let that embarrass you or you will act despicably from your own anger. Let it humble you instead, let it make you feel blessed and lead you to understand the responsibility that places on you. Perhaps you have a good heart, which in leading a people is as good as a strong mind. Foster that and then maybe you will be able to take this place. Because taking is one thing, holding quite another.

DIDI: Lovely speech, Mother. Also your last.

CATHERINE: And if you do not know the why, you will make a disaster of the how.

DIDI: Sister, are you with me? After what she did to you.

NATALIE: Your generals are not here, are they?

DIDI: I think they're a bit late. Yes.

GENERAL: A little, yes.

NATALIE: They are a bit late and a lot imprisoned.

   Beat.

CATHERINE: I have neglected you shamefully, Didi. For instance, the key to a good coup is secrecy, my darling son, and handing out portraits with the inscription the new Emperor Didi on them does not further that cause.

   Beat.

DIDI: So can I still do the coup?

CATHERINE: No.

DIDI: Oh.

CATHERINE: You must go now, Didi. To the summer house in Odessa. Stay there and read a while.

DIDI: Read? You're arresting me?

CATHERINE: You will try this again and Russia is too precious to be left to the fates of idiot sons of the aristocracy. It has always been my position.

DIDI: I am your son!

CATHERINE: I know, and I have not loved you nearly enough. We both will suffer that, but Russia will not. Orlo, if you will.

He leads DIDI *and the* GENERAL *out.*

NATALIE: We should go, we will be late.

CATHERINE: Of course.

CATHERINE *stops for a beat.*

NATALIE: What is it?

CATHERINE: I will die soon, and I will not have done enough.

NATALIE: Let's go.

She takes CATHERINE*'s hand. They exit.*

THE END

Also available from Currency Press

The Serpent's Teeth: Citizens and Soldiers
Daniel Keene
In *Citizens*, the humanity of ordinary people is stretched to the limit as they endeavour to survive in a land torn apart by war. In *Soldiers*, although the theatre of war is far from home, its impact on life can be just as devastating.
ISBN 978 0 86819 838 5

Toy Symphony
Michael Gow
Roland Henning has writer's block. When he tries to explain the situation to his therapist, his story begins to tumble back and forth between his childhood in Sydney's Sutherland Shire and his subsequent work as a playwright. His story is funny, fiercely eloquent and shockingly honest.
ISBN 978 0 86819 828 6

The Female of the Species
Joanna Murray-Smith
Margot Mason, celebrated feminist, academic, mother and author of the best-selling *The Cerebral Vagina*, has never had any problems with inspiring adulation. As she sits in her country home, in walks Molly Rivers, student and idealist. Initially flattered, Margot is less pleased when Molly handcuffs her to her desk and threatens to kill her. This deliciously funny farce looks at the fallout for the fans when our celebrated heroes change their mind.
ISBN 978 0 86819 825 5

Riflemind
Andrew Upton
John was once the frontman in one of the world's biggest bands, Riflemind. Now John and his wife Lynn are safe from the world in their walled country house. Money and anonymity, however, won't protect them from themselves or their past. As a comeback tour nears, a weekend of music-making is planned. As soon as the band and associated spouses, lovers and hangers-on arrive, it's a rock'n'roll circus. A darly comic and provocative play.
ISBN 978 0 86819 823 1

Visit Currency Press' new website now:

- Buy your books online
- Browse through our full list of titles, from plays to screenplays, books on theatre, film and music, and more
- Choose a play for your school or amateur performance group by cast size and gender
- Obtain information about performance rights
- Find out about theatre productions and other performing arts news across Australia
- For students, read our study guides
- For teachers, access syllabus and other relevant information
- Sign up for our email newsletter